For Lisa and Seamus

Aunts Up the Cross

ROBIN DALTON

Foreword by Clive James

VIKING

Viking
Penguin Books Australia Ltd
487 Maroondah Highway, PO Box 257
Ringwood, Victoria 3134, Australia
Penguin Books Ltd
Harmondsworth, Middlesex, England
Penguin Putnam Inc.
375 Hudson Street, New York, New York 10014, USA
Penguin Books Canada Limited
10 Alcorn Avenue, Toronto, Ontario, Canada M4V 3B2
Penguin Books (N.Z.) Ltd
Cnr Rosedale and Airborne Roads, Albany, Auckland, New Zealand
Penguin Books (South Africa) (Pty) Ltd
5 Watkins Street, Denver Ext 4, 2094, South Africa
Penguin Books India (P) Ltd
11, Community Centre, Panchsheel Park, New Delhi 110 017, India

First published by Anthony Blond Ltd 1965
Second edition published by Sun Books 1967
Reprinted by The Macmillan Company of Australia Pty Ltd 1980
New edition by William Heinemann Australia 1997
This edition published by Penguin Books Australia Ltd 1998

10 9 8 7 6 5 4 3 2

Typeset in Galliard
Printed and bound in Australia by Australian Print Group, Maryborough
Victoria

National Library of Australia
Cataloguing-in-Publication data:

Dalton, Robin.
  Aunts up the Cross.
  ISBN 0 670 88305 0.
  I. Title.
A823.3

www.penguin.com.au

ENDPAPERS: (*standing, left to right*) Barnett Keith-Cohen; Harry Morris-Cohen;
John J. Cohen ('the Judge'); Great-aunt 'Bertie'; Great-uncle 'Spot'; Dora; Sammie;
Great-uncle Luke (*seated adults*) Great-aunt Lilla; Great-aunt Flo; Great-aunt Juliet;
Jacob Hollander; my great-grandfather; Great-aunt Mina; Great-aunt Netta; Great-
aunt Anys (*children*) Colyn; Keneth; Colleen; Cedric; Lyndall

PAGE ii: Robin, aged about two.

FOREWORD by Clive James

B y the time I at last met Robin Eakin personally, on the *sable d'or* of Biarritz in the early eighties, she was called Robin Dalton and had been one of the most influential literary agents in London for half her career. We were introduced by our mutual friend, Michael Blakemore, whose talents as a director extend to real life: wherever he is, the stage teems with creative people, and in those years, in Biarritz every summer, there was always enough prominent human material spilling out of his house and down to the beach for everyone present to have begun a *roman-à-clef* except the novelists, who were already writing about what happened the *previous* summer. John Cleese and Michael Frayn came to the house to work on films and scripts; Tim Piggot-Smith came there to be obscure for a while after starring as Merrick in *The Jewel in the Crown*; and that trim form under the big straw hat, watching the children play in the shallows of the advancing tide, belonged to the exquisite Nicola Pagett.

But there was never any doubt who was the *grande dame* of the scene. It was Robin. She had a cut-glass accent that you would have sworn had been first turned and chiselled in the nurseries of Belgravia. I was relishing her company long before I realised that she was Australian, that she was Robin Eakin, and that she had once written a classic book. I had never even heard of *Aunts Up the Cross*, which sounded to me like a feminist tract about capital punishment in ancient Rome. When I read it, I realised that it was a prize example of a genre I had been looking for: the small Australian book that was better written than the big ones, the actual fragment of *echt* literature with a small 'l' that would make me feel less unpatriotic about all those behemoths of Literature with a capital 'L' which had been failing to convince me for so long. My party-piece recitative based on the opening page of *The Aunts Story* had been making me feel guilty for years. (I used to get a big laugh on the one-line paragraph 'And stood breathing' but I always felt ashamed: perhaps it only *sounded* ludicrous.) After I read *Aunts Up the Cross* the guilt vanished. Here at last was the living proof that a civilized, unpretentious, fully evocative prose style had been available in Australia ever since the young Robin Eakin handed in her first school essay. All we had ever needed to do was look in the wrong place. As so often happens, the true art was filed under entertainment.

To say that *Aunts Up the Cross* is beautifully written risks making the book sound like a filigree. It is anything but. Social information, moral judgement, comic action and tragic incident are all packed into sentences which have the density of uranium and would also have its weight, if they were not so proportionately constructed that they take off from the page like gliders picked up off a hill by a thermal from its face. Soon you, the lucky first-time reader of this marvellous little creation, will be in the light yet firm grip of its opening paragraph. Before that happens, let us analyse its first two sentences, because there will be no chance to do so once the third sentence reaches back to draw you on. Study this, you upcoming, unreliable memoirists: study this and weep.

> My Great-aunt Juliet was knocked over and killed by a bus when she was eighty-five. The bus was travelling very slowly in the right direction and could hardly have been missed by anyone except Aunt Juliet, who must have been travelling fairly fast in the wrong direction.

It's the gift that money can't buy and no amount of literary ambition can ever find a substitute for: the prose that sounds as if it is being spoken by the ideal speaker. Yet the spontaneity is all designed: 'very slowly' is exactly balanced against 'fairly fast', 'right direction' against 'wrong direction', and the impetus would be ruined if an editor—as almost any magazine editor nowadays would, especially if asked not to— were to insert an otiose comma after 'right direction'. The whole book is as precisely calculated as that, with the result that calculation scarcely seems to enter into it. When you get to the end, however, you find that Aunt Juliet and the bus make contact again, and you realise that you have been led a dance—a dance in a circle that might have been choreographed by Poussin, if Poussin had ever lived in the King's Cross area of Sydney.

Robin Eakin did live there, in that unlikely Arcadia. When I was growing up after the war, King's Cross was featured in the newspapers and magazines—not yet subsumed under the collective name of The Media—as Sydney's Montmartre, Schwabing, Soho and Greenwich Village, a reputation which seemed mainly to be based on the occasional appearance in the streets of Rosaleen Norton weighed down by mascara, sometimes as late as 11.30 in the evening. When Robin Eakin was growing up there before the war, King's Cross, for her family at any rate, spelt something more interesting than any Bohemia— gentility in reduced circumstances. She grew up in a house full of life; a house full of lives. In that nest of gentlefolk—Turgenev is one of the many names with whom she can be mentioned in the same breath—there was drama on every floor. *The Madwoman of Chaillot* was being staged on the mezzanine. *Les monstres sacrés* inhabited the verandah. No wonder she has spent so much of her time in and around theatres: she was born in one. She revelled in it. For her, Heaven was other people. She shames me in that regard. When I look back at my own book of memoirs, I see that its first critics were right: there is only one character in it, and everyone else is a walk-on. *Aunts Up the Cross* is just the opposite: its only half-realised character is the author herself.

If the book has a fault, that's it. When she casually lets slip that she had read all the major novels of Merdith before she was twelve years old, you want to know everything else about her education, and there is nothing like enough about the young love life of a woman so striking in her maturity. Though her evocation of Sydney in the war years ranks with the on-leave passages of T.A.G. Hungerford's *The Ridge and the River*, you can't help feeling that her American service personnel are miraculously well behaved. But the book was written in what was still an age of reticence, and the upside of that is better than the downside: where tact rules, frankness really startles, and no text of such brevity ever had so many flashpoints of shock. Aunt Juliet making contact with the bus is the very least of them. I mention no more because nothing should be allowed to dissipate the economy with which every telling vignette and intermezzo is prepared and resolved. I only say that the moment when the author's mother causes the death of the plumber is one of the great throwaway paragraphs in modern Australian letters. Read it, and then imagine how Xavier Herbert would have thrown it away. He would have thrown it away like an old refrigerator full of house-bricks: it would have taken him a hundred pages plus.

Aunts Up the Cross is all over in two hundred pages minus. A fan's foreword should show the same regard for brevity, so I will back out with one last unreliable memory before her reliable ones begin. I think it was while we were walking along the esplanade of the Côte des Basques (by which I mean we could equally have been in the drawing-room of her holiday-home maisonette, but I would rather you heard waves in the background) that I upbraided her for having written no more than this one perfect book. She fobbed me off with another drink—all right, it *was* the drawing-room—and politely neglected to state the obvious, which was that she had written something so sensitive to its own past, and so responsive to its own present, that it contained its own future. All the books she might have written later were already in it. What she was too modest even to think was that all the books the rest of us wrote later are in it too.

London 1996

PREFACE

My great-aunts, half of whom I never met in their lifetime, have sustained me throughout mine. In childhood with laughter, in adulthood with the recollections that gave birth to this book. Although only supporting characters in the fabric of those recollections, without them the singular nature of my family structure might have lacked the resonance which propelled me into recording it. So the four single aunts who never spoke to me during their lives are here still chattering on, and would not take kindly to the fact that they are doing so through the medium of this little memoir. In fact, they would hate it.

Twice, it has been published accidentally—neither driven nor suggested by me. So for those occasions I feel I owe them no apology. But perhaps I do for this third issue—not only condoned but instigated by me and with the added indignity of their photographs substantiating their existence. I quite obviously have not invented them.

I came to record them and the rest of the family because of my husband's death at thirty-three while undergoing one of the first open-heart operations. A doctor, he had published one book under a pseudonym and was at the time halfway through an autobiographical novel based on our marriage. 'If I die having this operation,' he said, 'will you finish the book?' This seemed logical to me, and easy, so I made the promise.

After his death I fled wintry England with my two small children, fourteen months and three, to a calm haven in Italy. I failed to finish Emmet's book but managed to write a diary for my children should I, too, die young. This is that diary.

It sat, yellowing in a drawer and forgotten, for seven years. One night, by then an established literary agent in London, I was at a cocktail party sharing a drink with publisher Anthony Blond. 'Why do you never send me anything?' he asked.

Mellowed by champagne, searching my mind for an unencumbered manuscript, I told him I didn't have any books. 'All I can think of is a fragment, which could be a play, I think, written by a dotty woman I went to school with.'

Anthony drove me home, demanded the pages

before he left and after finding them and handing them over, I forgot them.

Two days later Anthony rang. 'Where is this woman? She's got to finish this book.' Panic set in. 'Oh, Anthony. She'll never do that. She'll never write another word. She's Australian. She's mad.' We argued for some minutes, Anthony accusing me of odd behaviour for a literary agent, and finally announcing his intention to publish it as it stood—stands still today—hedging his bets with large margins, illustrations and thick paper, hopefully giving it the illusion of substance; I protesting that he couldn't possibly publish 22 000 words as a book.

Eventually, I gave in and signed a deal over a delightful lunch in the garden of his office. Anthony asked me at last for the name of this untraceable, intractable, mad woman. I confessed. I became a reluctant Blond author. I changed no identities, not thinking a copy would ever reach Australia, in my mind carelessly consigning it to the equivalent of a publisher's bottom drawer.

I am happy, though, that it was a success for Anthony—remained in print for a respectable time—did not, I hope, offend too many people, except for the remaining aunts, and that I managed to hide under my maiden name so that all the wonderful writers who seemed to value my opinions as their agent would never see me exposed.

Fifteen years passed. I began, with some timidity, to

confess to a very few people that I had written a book. Safely out of print, my exposure could not be too widespread.

Among my clients was the dramatist, Ben Travers, then in his nineties—three plays running in the West End of London, and still standing on his head for Michael Parkinson in TV interviews—a companion in laughter at our weekly dinners. He asked me about my Australian childhood. I gave him the old book, and he became its devotee. Many London publishers were vying for his autobiography, which I was urging him to write. He reluctantly agreed to do so on one condition—that whoever published his book must also re-issue mine.

I did not mention, nor consider, this when extracting bids from publishers for Ben's book and when the best bid came in from Jeffrey Symmons of W H Allen, Ben and I were taken to a clinching and celebratory lunch by Jeffrey. When we rose from the table at its jolly close, flushed with wine and achievement, Ben clutched my hand. 'You've told him the condition?'

Jeffrey's glow diminished somewhat. 'Condition?' he asked nervously. As Ben disclosed it, his glow disappeared entirely. Poor Jeffrey, desperately embarrassed and in the kindest tone he could muster, said, 'Robin, I didn't know *you* had written a book.' He saw the Travers manuscript drifting away from him; or encumbered by a nasty adjunct.

But, miraculously, it appeared that *Aunts* had been Jeffrey's snatched bedside reading for some years. Glow back, we all three strolled back to the W H Allen offices for a conference with the marketing manager—Jeffrey now with not one, but two prospective authors. I was asked if I thought the book would have any sales potential in Australia. I had been sent, in addition to a steady trickle of 'fan' letters over the intervening years since publication, a copy of an advertisement from an Australian newspaper placed by one Max Harris, seemingly the proprietor of a chain of bookshops, proudly announcing a coup. He had unearthed fifty copies of *Aunts Up the Cross*—one copy per person only; first come, first served. This appeared ample proof of demand.

The marketing manager was delighted. Max Harris was not only known to him but was something of a literary guru in Australia and his endorsement would influence the number of copies printed. A letter was dispatched asking him for this. Ben was sent home to write a preface to the new edition, and I to update it in minor details.

Two weeks later came the reply from Max Harris: '*Aunts Up the Cross* was a good little book in its day but no one would buy a copy now.' Apologies and embarrassment from Jeffrey; indignation from Ben; a shrug of shoulders from me; and abandonment of publication from the marketing division.

A year or so passed. Ben's book was published. I

went to Australia to produce a film. While there I read two articles by Max Harris in which he extravagantly praised my book and lamented its unavailability. This time curiosity overcame indifference. I tracked Max Harris down in England, where he was a literary adviser to Macmillan. A wary voice answered the phone. I stammered an introduction, explained my bewilderment over his articles in view of his effective blocking of its chances of reissue by W H Allen. Wariness turned to curtness. 'I'm hardly likely to encourage another publisher when you haven't bothered to answer all the letters we at Macmillan have written to you over the years asking if we might republish.'

Needless to say, no letters had been forwarded from old addresses but, contact made, I was published for the second time by Macmillan, which enjoyed as much success as Blond had and who swore the book would never fall from its back list.

It did. I hope that Penguin Books Australia, with this new edition, may entertain a new generation of readers. Now, thirty-two years later, with no writer clients to worry about, I can discard my 'Eakin' disguise and graduate from maiden name to that by which they knew me.

This edition has been slightly added to and amended but, as I have not attempted further updating, I beg the indulgence of readers in giving my viewpoint on such things as the state of the Australian theatre, remembering that this was first written in 1965. The book and I have become something of period pieces together.

Robin Dalton, 1997

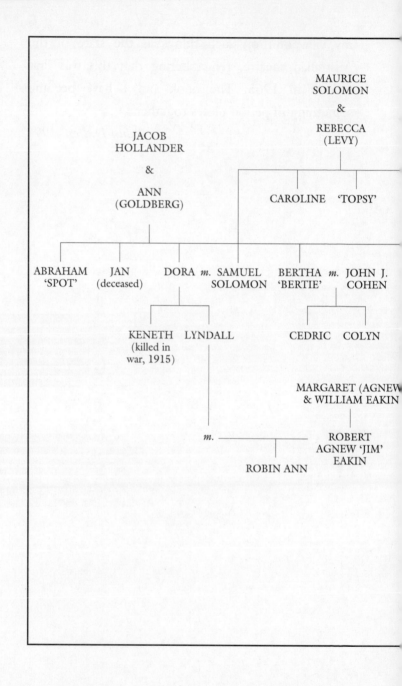

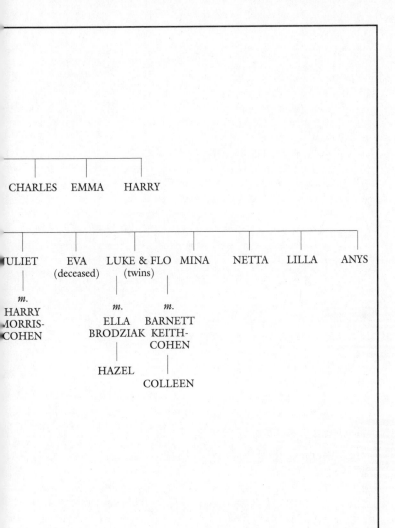

CHARLES   EMMA   HARRY

JULIET   EVA   LUKE & FLO   MINA   NETTA   LILLA   ANYS
              (deceased) (twins)
  | | |
  m.   m.   m.
HARRY   ELLA   BARNETT
MORRIS-   BRODZIAK   KEITH-
COHEN   COHEN
                           | |
                        HAZEL |
                               COLLEEN

CHAPTER 1

My great-aunt Juliet was knocked over and killed by a bus when she was eighty-five. The bus was travelling very slowly in the right direction and could hardly have been missed by anyone except Aunt Juliet, who must have been travelling fairly fast in the wrong direction. It was Aunt Juliet's habit, in addition to confusing the simpler rules of road safety, to wear dark glasses outdoors, winter and summer. This, being winter, probably contributed to the surprise advent of the bus. I think she wore the spectacles for the same reason that she often wore my mother's black osprey and jet hat and old silver fox jacket in bed. This was an alarming sight for visitors who, not finding other evidence of eccentricity in Aunt Juliet, felt the strain of accepting her get-up as normal. The hat and the foxes and the spectacles were all part of a behaviour pattern which I can only attribute to a strongly developed magpie instinct. Aunt Juliet was both rich and foolishly generous, but she was untiring in her efforts to gather and hold fast to her person crumbs from poorer tables. She bullied my mother for years for the hat and the cape and, although my mother was attached to both, Aunt Juliet wore her out in the end. The dark glasses she had found, in the street. She was also particularly attached to her diseased and removed appendix, which reposed in a nest of gall-stones in a small spirit bottle on the second shelf of the china cabinet in my grandmother's drawing-room. Until the appendix joined the Crown Derby and Wedgwood and Chelsea, I loved, as a child, to play with the china farmyard animals on the bottom shelf, but I could never go happily to the cabinet after Aunt Juliet's operation.

Aunt Juliet never seemed unusual to me: she fitted perfectly into the framework of the family. Her untimely end might have been dramatic in a family more given over to quieter leave takings. But, in ours, it just seemed natural. My mother always told me that we virtually killed Uncle Harry, Aunt Juliet's husband. He was visiting us from the country, where he and Aunt Juliet lived, when he fell through our dining-room floor and broke his neck. The dining-room was on the ground floor, but the foundations of the house allowed for a good six foot drop and when we discovered white ant in the floor and the builders took it up, nobody thought to tell Uncle Harry not to go into the dining-room. Great-uncle Spot fell off a ladder when changing a light bulb, and Great-uncle Luke tipped over backwards in his office chair. I don't know what their injuries were, but to my childish mind I remember that effect pretty soon followed cause and they died. In addition to Spot and Luke, there had been ten girls in my grandmother's family, of whom she was the eldest—but one, named Eva, died as a child from eating green apples, and an older sister, Jan, from blowing up a balloon. These were the tales told me by my grandmother and I accepted them.

Life in her family was richly and robustly lived: so it always seemed to my fascinated ears—and I would reflect with envy on those twelve busy lives humming away under a communal roof. But it was not only the

attraction of family life for my solitary childhood that invested my grandmother's family with fantasy and glamour. Looking back from the midst of my own ordinary adult life, it seems to me that a vein of quite extraordinary eventfulness enlivened the everyday existence of my mother's and father's lives and the lives of all my numerous great-aunts and -uncles and grandparents.

My great-grandfather was a Polish Jew, descended from generations of distinguished and learned rabbis. After the partition of Poland, he escaped military conscription in the Russian Army by swimming the Vistula on the eve of his fifteenth birthday. The story was vivid enough in its details as told to me by my grandmother up to this point. I could visualise the moonlight glinting on the dark water—hear the cries of the sentries on the banks—feel the panic of my great-grandfather when his companion swimming beside him in the dark was shot by the sentries and drowned. From the moment he climbed out safe on the Austrian bank, either her interest or mine must have waned, for I can recall nothing of his subsequent

Nana in middle age (*c.* 1912)—one of the many poses which were in those days handed out as visiting cards.

flight across Europe to England; of his meeting there at what must have been a much later date with my great-grandmother; or of the means by which he appeared many years later as a prosperous advertising executive and property owner in Australia. My grandmother was a young girl at the time of the family's move to Australia, but she seemed never to have been conscious of a time when they were not rich; and so the flight from Poland cannot have been entirely unsubsidised. The Australia she came to at the age of twelve was a country where fortunes were to be made out of land. Most of my great-grandfather's contemporaries settled in the bush and laid the foundations of sheep and cattle empires. My great-grandfather started in billboard advertising and his hoardings stretched in an unbroken line of posters on either side of his mile drive from his house to his office. The space thus acquired for display was the nucleus of a small kingdom in property.

The house in which they lived, Maramanah, was a sprawling, grey, turreted and balconied edifice. The five of the twelve children who survived and married

My mother, Lyndall, in her teens (*c.* 1910).

brought home their own growing families to the house and to their now widowed father, and the impressions I formed of life there were emphasised by family group photographs taken in the ballroom, with the background of drapes and aspidistra; of the family orchestra—my grandmother, regal and beautiful in grey satin and pearls, straddling a harp, and Aunt Juliet, hair *en pompadour*, her pretty mouth pursed round a flute. Each child started the piano at four, the violin at seven, and a third instrument at twelve. Melba was known to sing at their musical evenings, and any visiting or resident musician of note would spend a great deal of their time in Sydney at Maramanah.

My mother always hated life at Maramanah, endlessly quarrelling with her younger aunts who were both jealous and unmarried. The four elder girls were either mellowed by marriage into softer moulds or were by nature easier to live with. Their husbands were all, in bearing and repute, substantial characters

---

Maramanah, around the late 1920s. Now the site of the Fitzroy Gardens and the El Alamein fountain, the name surely a thorn in the dead flesh of my Jewish great-aunts. (Mitchell Library, State Library of New South Wales)

but, stationed as they were in innumerable family photographs amid the lace flounces of their joint spouses and sisters-in-law, they resembled so many currants on a richly iced cake. They had an air of being hired for the occasion and being suitably supplied with their frock coats, their stiff high collars and goatee beards as window-dressing for the undulating patterns of rounded arms, bosoms, and upswept curls of the ladies by whom they were outnumbered.

Sometimes they were pictured on bicycles, in stiff-fronted blouses, frilly pantaloons, buttoned boots, and boaters. Or with parasols, draped against the pillars of Maramanah's front porch. Whatever the scene, the photographer was on hand to record it, and the family obviously took its pleasures *en masse*. When the children were born, they were dotted here and there holding a solitary rose in one hand and the hand of the nearest aunt or uncle in the other.

My grandmother insisted that all the male members of her family had been either rabbis or judges for generations past, and that anything to do with 'trade' was an unthinkable occupation. The girls did indeed seem to live up to this ideal in their choice of husbands, either by intent, accident, or influence.

Aunt Bertie, next in age to my grandmother, married a judge of the High Court, a handsome and benign old man to whom Aunt Bertie always referred as 'the Judge'. The Judge was, like all true Australians, addicted to horse-racing. As he could not telephone through his bets from the court room to his illegal starting-price bookmaker, he would slip off his wig, and out the back door of the law courts to his contact man on the corner to place his half sovereign under the *nom de plume* of 'Mr John'. In addition to Aunt Bertie's judge, there were Aunt Flo's 'Barley', a barrister and brother to the Judge, and Aunt Juliet's Harry, who was a solicitor. My grandfather was City Treasurer, smacking ignobly of money, but at least he didn't sell things, nor did he make much.

Aunt Flo, Aunt Bertie, my grandmother and Uncle Luke produced a child or two apiece, and with this meagre supply of contemporaries my mother grew up

---

FOLLOWING PAGES: On the back porch of Maramanah (*c.* 1908), no doubt warming up for a musical evening, as Dame Clara Butt and her brood are the central characters. Nana, as always, stands out, because she is the only one of the sisters in dark clothing.

in the big grey house—the children's lives dominated
by the musical evenings and inevitable wranglings of a
complex network of aunts and uncles. The evenings
took place in the ballroom: it had one round side, and
a stage, aspidistra in pots, and chandeliers; it was the
heart of the house. At night there was always a
concert; by day there was always an aunt practising.
They, the husbands, were also expected to participate
in the concerts, but none of them were quite musical
enough to be relied upon to come in on the right beat.
The Toy Symphony was a particular disappointment
to Spot who had triumphantly brought home an
assortment of mechanical cuckoos and various birds
for the husbands to manipulate, but no amount of
rehearsals could bring them into synchronisation. I
knew, too, that the entrance hall had a marble floor,
for my mother had split her skull on it after sliding
down the banisters and this was always held up to me
as a horrid example. It had the effect of making me
long for a marble hall. The house had originally been

Great-aunt Bertie and 'the Judge'. A street photographer in
the 1930s has captured their stature, but not Bertie's jovial
nature. She has not enjoyed being 'snapped'.

beautiful, and Georgian. Its turrets and towers and balconies had been added by my great-grandfather, as had later lavatories. In my mother's childhood, space had stretched only to a boys' and a girls' lavatory, each one having a throne, and beside it a row of chamber pots so that after breakfast was a friendly time of communal squatting.

This tribal existence was disrupted by the death of my great-grandfather who, though dying quietly in my grandmother's arms, managed to invest the act with the modicum of required family drama by doing it suddenly and on the chaise longue which is now in my own bedroom and which was always known in my childhood as 'the couch my darling daddy died on'. My grandmother told me that he was reading *Uncle Vanya* when he died, but I never liked to enquire about this hitherto unmentioned uncle as she was always tearful telling me this tale and I thought that Uncle Vanya must have upset the family dreadfully and in all probability had caused my great-grandfather's death.

(*left to right*) My maternal grandmother, Dora; son, Keneth; husband Sammie; and Lyndall—some of the entities under Maramanah's roof.

After he died, the married children dispersed into houses of their own. My mother was thus freed from the constant company of her maiden aunts, and after she married my father she never spoke to them again. The official reason given was that she had married outside her religion, but I think old animosities had fastened on any excuse. My father was a Northern Irish Presbyterian raised by a stern but loving mother, to whom he broke the news in some trepidation that he wished to marry a Jewess.

'Son,' said my Irish grandmother, 'I don't care if you marry a Negress as long as she isn't a Catholic.' (Years later, my own husband's Catholic family did not speak to me, his Presbyterian wife, until our daughter was nearly a year old.)

CHAPTER 2

The four maiden great-aunts whose acquaintance I was thus denied were a source of endless merriment in our family. In addition to their reputedly unlovable natures, their parents had given them the names Lilla, Mina, Netta, and Anys. These my father gleefully referred to as Litter, Titter, Fritter and Anus. My mother's epithet for them became, at the time of the Palestinian troubles, the Stern Gang.

My parents' courtship and meeting were rakish rather than romantic. My father was quite startlingly handsome, six feet four inches and, in the naval uniform he was wearing at the time he met my mother, a sight to turn heads and attract all eyes. She first saw him in a tram, rattling up William Street.

I suppose she stared: he winked at her, and she, blushing guiltily, flounced off the tram. That night she was introduced to him at a dance at Government House. He then invited her to come and watch him dance in a charity pageant, in which six young blades and six young debutantes were taking part. My mother went: she sat in the front row. My father was drunk and had obviously not attended any of the rehearsals. While the other eleven were pointing their left feet, he was pointing his right, and again winking at my mother: when they turned to the left, he turned to the right. In addition, he had his satin knee breeches on back to front and the plume from his hat hung over one eye and he had to keep blowing it away in order to see.

Well, she married him, and eighteen years later, I was asked to appear in a tableau in a similar pageant in aid of the same charity, organised by the same society matron. She was a rather imposing lady, of theatrical background, who had married well into wealth and social position but who retained her old connection with the theatre by organising whatever charitable theatrical entertainment she could, and by attending

My father during the First World War.

every first night of the Sydney theatre in a series of
coloured wigs. This multi-hued entrance invariably
stole the show and my father described her as a 'female
ham who can't be cured'. She had a formidable
memory, however, and when I presented myself with
my eleven young companions at her ornate Italianate
villa for our first rehearsal, she admonished me sternly.
'I hope, my child, that you will behave yourself better
than your father did twenty years ago.'

After my parents' marriage they, in their turn, went
to live with my grandparents in a smaller house where
they remained—my parents on the top floor and my
grandparents on the ground floor—for thirty-five
years. After the first year my father never spoke to my
grandmother. This, too, I accepted as perfectly normal
behaviour. He remained on friendly terms with my
grandfather, and he even tolerated Aunt Juliet for
whom, after Uncle Harry's death, a special suite of
rooms was built on what had been a flat roof halfway
up the stairs, and which was known thereafter as the
'mezzanine floor'—or, as photographs of dead
relatives grew in number, the 'mausoleum'. Aunt
Juliet was frightened of him, but she would defiantly
say, 'Good morning, Jim' if trapped on the stairs.
When my father, who was a doctor, left the house on

his rounds each morning my grandmother and great-aunt would come scurrying up the stairs to my mother and there they would stay until they heard his key in the door downstairs. This arrangement suited me beautifully as a child: I was the focal point of two separate and complete loving households under the one roof, and what the one could not or would not provide for me in the way of attention or entertainment, the other could and did. Again, it was not until many years of contact with other humans had taught me that I learnt perhaps our family relationships were not usual: it was then I asked my father what had started his ancient battle with his mother-in-law.

'I found early in my married life,' he said, 'that I could not take my trousers off without turning round and finding your grandmother watching me.'

My poor mother was the buffer between these two constantly warring factions. Warm-hearted, impulsive and emotional, she suffered from the strain of keeping the peace whenever possible. Unfortunately she was seldom able to keep calm at the same time, and in no time at all she would be driven by my father to tears and by my grandmother to the limits of rage and exasperation. My grandmother interfered in every

small detail of her daughter's life, domestic as well
as marital, and where she could not physically poke
in a finger, she badgered with advice, criticism, and
unsolicited opinions.

The most violent and constant of these criticisms
revolved around my mother's determination never
to have me taught the piano. My grandmother
considered this an uncivilised deprivation, one notch
higher than being allowed to go out without gloves.
My mother, I learnt much later in life, had been a
brilliant pianist, playing duets with her adored, dead
brother and I expect by banishing music forever after
from her life, a raw wound was opened less frequently.
What was, to me, ancient, mellowed history was, in
reality, just four years past in her memory.

The wars between my father and grandmother,
however, were silent but not necessarily impassive and,
as my mother was the buffer, then I was the battlefield. Any injury to my small person was the signal for
immediate action, and the strategies resorted to by
both sides gave no thought to how ploughed the
battlefield might become in the struggle. A badly cut
knee meant for me hours of bandaging, strapping, and
applying of painful unguents by my grandmother; to
be followed by equally fierce stripping off of all

coverings by my father. This two-sided treatment would be repeated until my leg eventually healed despite it. What conflicts and neuroses were thus born in me I do not know; in retrospective reflection I enjoyed it enormously, was continuously stimulated, and my own children's lives, kept to routine and order at great inconvenience to myself, seem incomparably duller.

At the age of three I was sent to school, to a very superior establishment started by the Misses Cheriton, two middle-aged spinster sisters who had been private governesses and had acquired some sophistication but no business acumen. We moved school fairly frequently—I now suspect pursued by creditors—to a succession of charming houses, all renamed 'Doone' on our arrival, where it seems to me we lived on strawberries and cream and acquired an astonishingly liberal education for the Australia of the twenties. It is to them that I owe the fact that I saw Pavlova dance the Swan: we four and five year olds were bundled off to a matinée, and some dim memory of the magic remains.

I was dressed in the height of (French) fashion from birth. I particularly remember the tissue-wrapped red winter coat arriving from Paris which I, aged four, hated wearing because it was so beautiful and therefore different from all the other children. Around its collar and hem were appliquéd daisies, cut out of the same material, and I was made, until I rebelled, to wear it to school.

At home I was educated by my grandmother, who talked and talked. Her talk was directed at me, relentlessly. It was not conversation: no response was required. How I squirmed and sighed with resignation at those oft-repeated maxims with which she sought to increase my daily store of wisdom, and with what little shocks of recognition do I realise their truth as instances along the paths of later life have caused me to stumble over one. When she disapproved of one of my companions it was, 'If you lie down with dogs, you'll get up with fleas.' When I protested against the futility of doing something for a lost cause, she protested, 'Every little helps, as the old lady said when she spat into the sea.' When I kicked against the unreasonability of some of her taboos she told me, 'Reason always means what someone else has got to say.' And, most frequent of all, was her rejoinder to my

---

Me, sulkily wearing the red Parisian coat, with Nannie Bradley.

complaints against her 'nagging'—'Never mind! If I throw enough mud, some of it is bound to stick.' What fascinated, though mystified, me most, however, was, 'A stitch in time saves nine, as the mother of eight said as she sewed up the front of her husband's pyjamas.'

Into her talk, too, came her favourite literary characters: Peggotty, from *David Copperfield*, was as well known to me as one of the household; my mother's boundless optimism in the face of imminent, though small, financial doom was always dubbed 'Micawberism'. I thought this, and her other favourite, 'Malapropism', were probably to be found in the huge dictionary by her bed. But they had faces and characteristics for me—Peggotty, Mr Micawber and Mrs Malaprop were shadowy but permanent members of the family.

While she talked, Aunt Juliet tickled me for hours on end. The tickling is a family vice, the taste for which was passed on to me by my mother, but in the years since I have never found such an untiring and uncomplaining tickler as Aunt Juliet. On hot, sticky

Me, aged ten, in the gardens at Doone, inspired by Pavlova?

summer nights when I could not sleep, or had the toothache, Aunt Juliet sat by my bedside playing the 'game'. This was a geographical tour of my person: 'Quickly—England!' I would say when one foot sole—perhaps Italy— had become numb and tired of sensation, and Aunt Juliet's nimble fingers must go racing to the back of my neck. Only on one point did she insist as we changed countries every night—my bottom was Germany.

I had my own game with Aunt Juliet's person. This was the privilege and doubtful pleasure of being allowed to put my finger in the 'hole'. The hole was indeed a hole, of dark and mysterious depths, in the soft fat folds of her upper thigh. One day she and Uncle Harry were driving in one of the earlier motor cars to catch the Newcastle ferry. There was a collision with a horse and cart. The horse, cart, man, woman and child occupants and the car—Harry and Juliet, swathed in duster coats and motoring veils—sailed into the Hawkesbury River. Only Harry and Juliet were recovered, and whatever injury Juliet suffered had left the 'hole' as reminder.

My relationship with my other two married great-aunts was never as close as it was with Aunt Juliet. I only remember once visiting Aunt Juliet's house in

Newcastle before, when I was four, she came to live with us, but relics of her life there were scattered about the house. In my grandmother's silver cupboard a shelf was taken up with Aunt Juliet's silver menu holders and a stack of old menu cards. Aunt Juliet's married life had consisted largely of arranging flowers, writing her menus, and waking up Uncle Harry in the night to tickle her back. Uncle Harry was never known to protest at this indignity, and one wonders if any other marital rights were afforded him, as Aunt Juliet protested loudly and often that she had always been too frightened to have children.

A housekeeper, Doris, had been brought out from England by Juliet, trailing hinted-at glories of ducal households behind her. Doris, unaccountably, quietly, and eventually gave birth to a nameless child whose presence was explained by Aunt Juliet as the result of a day trip by Doris to Sydney. An aura of threatening and shadowy holocaust hung in my mind forever after about the train—known as the *Newcastle Flyer*—solid and encased in brass, mahogany, engraved glass and reclining seats, for surely it had played its part in Doris' downfall? The child was seldom mentioned. Aunt Juliet sailed blithely above the situation, resorting only once to indignation when Doris' name was billed before hers at the reading of Uncle Harry's will to the tune of thirty shillings a week for life.

Of the other two, Aunt Flo was pretty, pretentious and nearly as silly as Juliet: she didn't enter our lives as much as Aunt Bertie who, of all the sisters, was the only one resembling my grandmother in bigness of heart and spirit and in the forcefulness of her personality. Like all the sisters, she was large and fat and soft and, at the age when I first remember her, dressed only in black. When I think of her it is largely in connection with the food I had to eat in her house. Highly spiced cakes and brown cinnamon biscuits, Jewish fried fish, and a wonderful milky pea soup called 'peas and clice'. Aunt Bertie was always cooking or playing the piano: she would break off in the middle of a song to take something out of the oven, and I was allowed to strum on the piano and pop the hot biscuits into my mouth.

It was in Aunt Bertie's house that I absorbed the only atmosphere and customs of Judaism which I ever remember seeing. My grandparents seemed to have given up their religion, or at least the outward show of

My mother with a friend at Palm Beach in the height of 1930s fashion—the first beach pyjamas.

it, at the same time as their daughter and, except for the crisp squares of Matzo bread which arrived at every Passover but more for enjoyment than necessity, I don't remember any rituals or religious taboos. There certainly remained a half humorous superstition, which was never taken very seriously. My grandmother, an old lady whose normal outlook was panoramic in its tolerance, regarded these remnants of prejudice of hers much as one might regard an unsightly but long-accepted physical defect. She did not like the idea of baptism, so that when I was finally christened a Presbyterian at the age of four, I was sent to a Vaudeville show of very doubtful propriety with the cook immediately afterwards to take my mind off the ceremony and prevent me telling my grandmother about it with any degree of coherence. Despite the urgings and promptings of the cook, I would not, however, forget the main event—'the funny man in the black coat who threw water on me'. Her dislike of the Catholic religion was firmly planted: when I married a Catholic and she was forced to write about it in her letters to me she would never write the word, but denote its place on the page with a large black cross. But the dietary rules of Judaism had long since lost the battle with her appetite and love of good food.

But sometimes on Friday nights I was invited to the evening meal at Aunt Bertie's: her children and grand-children gathered round the table and Uncle John sat at the head with a small, round, black skullcap on his head, intoning a Hebraic chant which was to me wonderfully theatrical and exciting. Aunt Bertie had two sons: Cedric had married within the Faith and joined his father in wearing the black skullcap and bringing up his children in traditional Jewish fashion; Colyn had not, and had joined my mother in the shadows of family approval. At his occasional appear-ances at the Friday night gatherings, Colyn put a white napkin on his head instead; this reduced my cousin, Adrienne, and myself to fits of giggles for which we were invariably told to leave the room.

Aunt Bertie lived in a house just along the street from the most permanent of the Doone establish-ments, and it was this proximity which fostered my friendship with her. It was easy to slip over the fence and dash along to Aunt Bertie's for ten minutes—running back with pockets full of cookies for my playmates who were keeping watch.

The Doone girls were a socially favoured and exclusive little band. The Governor's daughter was my best friend and in exchange for afternoon teas at

Government House after school, I regularly beat her to pulp in the school yard. We all felt it to be a particularly English failing that her nose bled on these occasions, but poor Rosemary struggled bravely to shed her pretty accent and her frailties. She was also to be pitied because she was brought and fetched from school by the Vice-Regal car and chauffeur, while we were free to wander home at will across the streets and harbourside parks and up the steep stone steps from the water's edge to Kings Cross, and neighbouring Elizabeth Bay, where my walking companions lived. My mother was never nervous: the walk was a long one, so it seems Sydney was a safe and friendly place in which to grow up.

It was also a tight little world. Far from being a free and classless society in a new and vigorous culture, it was the concentrated quintessence of a snobbery and class-consciousness brought from the old. Our parents and our grandparents were friends: we met no-one at school outside this circle and, inside the circle, allowances were made for its members. Because my mother was of this world, it never occurred to me that her Jewishness might have been a cause for apartness and that there existed in the world outside Sydney an anti-Jewish prejudice. I think this must have been because a few Jews in Sydney had established themselves early in the social hierarchy. I am sure it never occurred to my mother, or to her second cousins, the Levy's, that theirs could have been a life of social ostracism. Australian Roman Catholics were not so lucky. I knew very few, except our cook, and one dear family friend. They were usually one's servants, invariably Irish and politically left wing, therefore posing a threat to our secure world.

However, although my school life and family friends followed an established Australian pattern, the life within the walls of our house certainly did not.

FOLLOWING PAGES: A Doone school group. Rosemary Game (*second row, first left*) sits next to me, despite the playground bashings.

CHAPTER 3

O ur house was the only private residence in Kings
Cross, the city's 'European' quarter—the
'Montmartre' of Sydney, people called it, with flattery
and nostalgia. Actually, it was fairly hideous; like all of
urban Sydney being a dusty hodgepodge of low-built
buildings, all in need of a coat of paint—the upper
halves flats and residential rooms and the lower halves
shops, offices and cinemas. Between the two, cutting
off the dirty stucco and dingy brickwork from the
glaring neon signs, were the ubiquitous iron or
concrete awnings, the most characteristic features of
Sydney's dim architecture.

Maramanah stood at the end of Darlinghurst Road,
our street, only two blocks away, but already on the
corner of a far smarter one, which led down to the

harbour's edge. At the other end, Darlinghurst Road joined a smaller, steeper and dustier street known, because of the preponderance of pimps and prostitutes among its inhabitants, as the Dirty Half Mile—or sometimes, but never by my grandmother, as Douche Can Alley. My grandmother referred to the girls as 'Soiled Doves'.

In front of our house was the only tree in the Cross, a broad and dusty-leaved plane-tree and, together with the house, it formed a small oasis of incongruous suburbia amid the glare and noise of the flashing signs, the foreign voices, the juke boxes and the cinema crowds. As a child, I drifted to sleep at the front of the house, immune to the noise ten feet below my window, although the voices, some of them familiar from greetings exchanged at my father's surgery door, drifted through my dreams, now remembered with the clarity of nursery rhymes. I particularly liked one of the standard approaches of the prostitutes to their customers: 'Thirty bob—strip to the earrings.' It had the familiar ring of the bookies' voices calling out their odds.

The house itself was really very small, I now realise, for the life it contained. It was a wonderful child's house, full of dark corners, hidden cupboards, unnecessary doors, delicious shiny, rounded banisters,

107 Darlinghurst Road before the front was extended to the street in about 1920: the beautiful iron balconies were later discarded, but the swing gate and porch together with the tree survived.

and two of those areas of waste space but endless possibility, the 'light areas'. There was both a flat roof, for laundry and sun-bathing and dolls' houses, and a sloping tiled one over the front half of the house for perilous climbs. There was a sheer drop of about sixty feet to be bridged when leaping to the fire escape of

the block of flats next door with the odious little
red-haired boy who lived in them, and there was,
surprisingly enough, no supervision or restriction on
these activities. It can only be that my father was busy,
my mother playing bridge, and the current servants
about their own business during these danger-fraught
forays, for I can certainly remember no admonitions
or warnings except my grandmother's with which I
fought a bitter and unceasing war, sure of paternal
backing for any amount of defiance.

Nevertheless, when these battles were over and I
had climbed down from roof, drainpipe or banister, it
was always to her drawing-room I went for the private,
secret place, which a child needs away from adult
household life. It was a long, low, dark, cool room,
whose windows looked out onto the feet of passers-by,
and like everything else touched by my grandmother
and Juliet in their seemingly constant and shared state
of bereavement, its colour scheme was in varying
shades of what they called 'heliotrope'. They both
started wearing this as half-mourning very early in

FOLLOWING PAGES: (*left*) Me awaiting the boy next
door in the back lane. (*right*) Me, posing, having enticed
him onto the roof, in one of my mother's kimonos.

their death-bespattered lives. My grandmother carried it into her furnishings with a certain amount of relief in the way of pale background chintzes and a grey cushion here and there. Juliet's bedroom was, on the contrary, a stretch of unbroken purple. Her heavy mahogany furniture, combined with this funereal grandeur, did indeed give added weight to the mausoleum-like effect created by the many photographs of the departed.

Death was always present, cosily accepted, in my life. The fairy tales I was told were the true and wonderfully stirring accounts of dead relations and how they had met their ends. The walls of the house were hung with their portraits and, indeed, so obscure was the relationship sometimes that I wonder if death alone was not sufficient reason for winning a place in my grandmother's life. The books I read had all belonged to her only son, my dead Uncle Ken, killed at Gallipoli, and his mournful, beautiful, twice life-size portrait hung above my head. His swords and caps and Oxford mufflers still hung in the hall. His books were all by dead authors—the life cycle of the comic serial with which my children live was unknown to me.

A war-time group: Keneth, Dora and Lyndall.

Uncle Ken didn't even die in action in the ordinary way. He was shipped back to England following a shrapnel wound; developed pneumonia and, one day, while my mother and grandmother were visiting him in the hospital, he asked for some bread and sugar— took one bite and died, leaving the imprint of his teeth in the sugar. My grandmother told me this sad story so many times, so graphically, that I could almost feel the gritting of the sugar on my own teeth, and certainly the thought of pneumonia always carries with it the association of that apparently fatal bite. I longed to ask her if Uncle Ken had had time to swallow it, but by this stage of the story, tears would be flowing freely down her face and I felt it somehow to be an unfitting and callous query. Our other favourite reading, which usually took place in her bedroom, were Uncle Ken's letters from Oxford, which she kept in a large trunk under her bed. One or two of these, never less than twenty pages long, were hauled out every day and read to me. She was determined that in some way I would absorb something of my uncle's thoughts and experiences. In addition to the trunk under the bed, a huge old edition of *Webster's Dictionary* sat on her bedside table from which she read two pages every night.

So my childhood life was sharply defined and varied

in my memory by the geography of the house. My grandmother's drawing-room where the china cabinet offered up its riches at one end and the book shelves at the other is most vivid in my mind. I found it both comforting and stimulating, and spent many hours curled up on the sofa steadily reading through my dead uncle's books. They were mostly books he had acquired at Oxford, and I suppose they reflected the undergraduate tastes of 1910–14: they passed indelibly into my child's mind and it never occurred to me to ask for anything lighter or more suitable for a five to twelve year old. I digested all of George Meredith, most of Thomas Hardy (inexplicably, at twelve, my favourite was *The Dynasts*), Ibsen, Charles Lamb, Maeterlinck (in French), a series of 'Lives of the Master Musicians' (Beethoven's was more thrilling to me than any schoolgirl romance—I still picture him perpetually roaring on a mountain top) and, for poets, Keats, Shelley, Dante Gabriel Rossetti and Browning. Self-involvement was utter in *The Mill on the Floss*. Maggie Tulliver was my heroine; I longed to have her thick, dark locks and fierce, lively eye, and I longed for a brother such as Tom. I was not lonely, but the closeness of relationship of the Tulliver family seemed to me such a satisfying and enriching condition compared to my store of second cousins, great-aunts and great-uncles, and the shadowy company of the dead. To satisfy my fantasies, when I was eight I wrote a book, neatly written and copiously illustrated, entitled 'My Relations'. I made gallant attempts to disguise the few and distant ones that I had under false names, but Aunt Juliet is there, to the life: 'She means well but she doesn't mean much', and the four maiden great-aunts concentrated into one—'I have an aunt whose single-blessedness has soured her to the world.'

Occasionally my grandmother invaded my privacy and then she would read aloud to me something she considered suitable for a small child, as a change from the letters and the dictionary. It was usually *Brer Rabbit* or *The Houseboat on the Styx*. Sometimes it was Pepys' diary and, when on my seventh birthday I was given a dog, a snapping little ginger Pomeranian, I called him Samuel Pepys in honour of my then favourite author.

Pepys was the only childhood pet I had, apart from a fierce galah in a cage. I think we tired of the galah fairly quickly (unless he tired of us and escaped) when my father failed in all attempts to teach him to imitate the bald parrot who lived on the Victorian–New South Wales border, in Albury railway station. He had two raucous calls in his repertoire, as one alighted from the train: 'Give me one more feather and I'll fly' and 'Stand back! I'm an eagle.' The galah, never to be dignified with a name, outstared my father, and stuck to his own contemptuous squawk.

These sayings, along with those of Samuel Pepys, permeated my childhood, jumbled up, the bird's cries merging with Pepys' admonitions to Mrs Pepys. No extra resonance was afforded them or the tunes and advertising slogans of the day—all of them became the stuff of vocabulary.

'I like Aeroplane Jelly' floated behind the little aeroplanes on banners as they patrolled the beaches. 'I like Aeroplane Jelly; Aeroplane Jelly for me. I like it for breakfast: I like it for tea. Aeroplane Jelly for me' floated out of the radio; on entering a country town by road, we were greeted by a large banner strung from telegraph pole to pole: 'Welcome to Leura—a good Rexona town'; on departure, a 'Farewell' replaced the welcome.

My grandmother's bedroom, where I lay listening to her stories, was the centre of a more active and gregarious life. Her dining-room was always a sinister room, redolent of Juliet's widowhood and thoughts of Uncle Harry, into which I seldom ventured. The

cupboard under the stairs had a tiny window and
loads of treasures, but here Rosa Toomey, the cook,
hung up her hat and coat and left her small suitcase
crammed with her life's savings in pound notes which
she brought to work every day; and so I had the
obscure feeling of being in forbidden territory.
Halfway up the stairs, Juliet's room was given over
entirely to Juliet's material comfort and possessions.
Dozens of dresses hung under their organdie covers,
and tray after tray slid out of the lowboy and the
tallboy packed with gloves, and scarves and under-
wear, all in their heliotrope organdie bags. The whole
house was stuffed with the haphazard acquisitions of
the Victorian and Edwardian middle-class family. In
the dark hall, one bumped into corners of substantial
carved camphor chests: inlaid brass ornaments, trays,
huge vases and gongs gleamed from every corner.
'Cloisonne ware' was a favourite lamp base: every glass
surface, however utilitarian, was heavily cut. I har-
boured the vague idea that glass was really called 'cut
glass', except when used in window panes. The
dressing-tables of my grandmother and Aunt Juliet
were a riot of silver angels and cherubs entwined and
garlanded around pots and jars and pin-trays, and
frolicking round the tops of cut-glass scent bottles.

On the walls hung perfectly hideous paintings—
brightly coloured sunsets and coy, long-haired ladies
simpering naked on the seashore—and an occasional
etching of some quite uninspiring building. Stored
away in drawers and in the camphor chests were
mounds of beautiful lace, Irish crochet jackets and
delicate shawl collars, salvaged from nightdresses and
blouses and former glories; silver reticules, and
discarded jet fringes.

Upstairs in my parents' domain, although I had my
own small bedroom there, life was so packed with
people and incident that no corner of it remains
privately mine in my memory. The life of our part of
the house revolved around the telephone—a wind-up
contraption with an operator at the other end—
constantly ringing for the doctor, and the snores of my
father trumpeting away through the noise. The hall at
the top of the stairs was large enough for a table, and
a few chairs, the telephone, another flight of stairs
leading to the servants' rooms, and a window opening
into the kitchen which faced the top of the stairs. This
window had no possible use as ventilation or light
entry, as there was another perfectly adequate window
in the kitchen opening onto the outside world, so my
mother must have had it knocked in the wall for freer

social intercourse. Whoever was working in the
kitchen could see who was coming up the stairs and
vice versa. The bottom two or three rows of stairs
leading to the maids' rooms were usually occupied as
chairs by visitors who could call through the kitchen
window to my mother, invariably making or drinking
tea. Later, she went even further and ripped the
kitchen door off its hinges as well. She did it herself,
which was a feat of some strength. Next to the kitchen
was the sole, over-worked bathroom, strategically
placed bang in the middle of this continually crowded
hall. When I was very small I remember there being a
key to the bathroom door, for I had one hated nannie
who locked me in the bathroom as punishment. But at
some period it was lost, for never after was there a key.
This created a situation in which any visit to our bathroom involved a feeling of insecurity and necessitated
a constant state of alertness.

As may be surmised, ours was a house in which the
feeling of being 'lived in' flourished to the exclusion of
all else. I suppose it must have been fairly shabby but
one didn't notice this amid the crush of people, the
cigarette smoke, and the constant preparation or
eating of food. My mother smoked nearly 100
cigarettes per day—there was not a piece of furniture
which had not been scarred by her butts—and, not in

the least house-proud, all her enormous energy and creativeness was focused on her kitchen. She never cooked until the war, and then when we were reduced to Rosa, increasingly cranky and growing older, and one maid, she attacked the business of cooking with gusto and joy. She was a natural chef—inventive and lavish. She was indifferent to her own comfort; the sofa would, and often did, do as well as her bed. She and my father shared a large dressing-room which was always littered with his clothes, and the only place in the house to which she could retire in an attempt at privacy was the unlockable bathroom. 'My idea of luxury,' she would say, 'is to be allowed to go to the lavatory by myself.' This seldom happened, as my grandmother hated to be shut out, and thought it was an unnatural and unfilial act.

There was nothing in the house forbidden to me. I was allowed to choose my own wallpaper and paint my own bedroom. One year, when I was about nine, I chose a bright, sick pink, and the next year an even brighter hospital green. Halfway round the skirting board, with only the fronts done of my chest of drawers and wardrobe, I would tire, and the painter would be called in to finish the job, but not until I had

FOLLOWING PAGES: Maramanah – my mother and younger cousin on the on the balcony circa 1907.

painted the lavatory seat in the year's favourite shade.

These twin themes dominating the house, of death and lack of privacy, merged and culminated in the unhappy event of my mother killing the plumber. At one end of the upper hall was the back door, normally left open for sun and air. One summer morning the servants were busy elsewhere, the house was for once empty, and my mother emerged naked from her dressing-room *en route* to take a bath. At that moment the plumber (he was a new one) came up the back stairs and met her on the landing. He promptly had a heart attack from which he never recovered. My mother always felt that the fact that death was not instantaneous detracted from the impact of her nudity and the dramatic possibilities of the story.

Although I was a solitary child in a house full of adults, the house was undeniably always full, and this variety of characters I knew intimately at an early age was a rich fund of entertainment. I remember Tony McGill, our starting-price bookmaker, who ate a pound of raw tripe every morning for breakfast. At the same meal, he was also apt to whip out his not inconsiderable male member, of which he was inordinately proud, and display it on a plate. Perhaps my father had embellished this story, perhaps Tony had boasted of having done it only once, but it made our own family breakfast appear a dull event to me.

Thursday was 'settling' day. Every Thursday night, Tony McGill came round to finalise the previous Saturday's betting. Tony had a special line in patter, which he had learnt from the then famous Fitzpatrick Travelogues. Something about the rich, resonant tones of Mr Fitzpatrick's voice and his choice of exotic sounding places impressed Tony. As he left with the week's takings he would wave to assembled company and call out in his ringing bookmaker's voice, 'Farewell to Calabadad, Land of Mysterious Women!'

Occasionally, if his visit was later than usual, my mother asked him to stay to dinner, but even in such an easygoing household as ours this was a risky move and apt to create tension. Flushed with whisky and bent on entertaining the party, Tony would go through his repertoire of Fitzpatrickisms and once having exhausted these, would feel that something more spectacular was expected of him. Another regular visitor was a genteel and aged governess of my mother's, Sally Thornton, who one night had the misfortune to sit next to Tony, casting around for fresh topics. When all else failed, his own body never ceased to fascinate him. He leapt to his feet, pushed

back his chair and, whipping his shirt out of his trousers, thrust his bare and hairy chest close to Sally's face.

'How's that?' he roared. 'Go on—have a feel—as hard as a rock and in the pink of condition.'

Sally leant across this offering and addressed herself, quivering with gentility, to Tony's other neighbour. 'Don't you feel, Mr Blackman,' she said, 'that Gilbert and Sullivan were antipathetic?'

Poor Tony could never understand the rebuff.

As frequent a visitor as Tony was Siddie Jacobs, a dim-witted car park attendant to whom my father would lend five pounds to be repaid at the rate of sixpence a week over the years. He was once caught chasing little girls and my father guaranteed his good behaviour to the police. Siddie was about five feet high. He lisped badly and wore a long, white coat flapping around his ankles. When my father felt particularly mischievous he would say to Siddie on his visits to the surgery, 'Go upstairs, Sid, and say hello to Mrs Eakin. She's not doing anything.'

My mother in a newspaper photograph taken at Warwick Farm races in the late 1930s. I remember the outfit: a Mainbocher brown-and-white-flecked wool.

As my mother invariably was doing something and, once up, Siddie was not easy to get down, this was not a popular move.

There was always a current 'lame dog' of my mother's in the house. There was the girl behind the cash desk at the butcher's shop opposite who suffered from a painful and recalcitrant boil on her behind. It was too far for her to travel to her home each day for the prescribed treatment and so she came at lunch-time and sat patiently in a bowl of boiling water and boracic on our bathroom floor while my mother served her delicious luncheons on a tray.

More disrupting were the resident visitors. During really full periods, my mother sometimes never slept in a bed for weeks at a stretch. One fruity-voiced gentle-man my parents met on a cruise lived with us for two years before disappearing with all the whisky and leaving behind a pile of unpaid bills. Shortly after his departure, my mother came home with a loathsome Viennese from her bridge club: I was turned out of my bedroom for him, and was incensed still further by the large framed photograph of himself kept on my bureau and the coronets embroidered on his underpants. It took nine months for us to convince my mother that, despite his excellence at the bridge table, he must go.

Not all our house guests, eating or sleeping, were

mistakes. One English theatrical producer whom my father invited to dinner remained in close harmony and affection—nightly—for seventeen years. Next to racing, the dominant influence in our lives was the theatre. The theatre in Sydney lapsed into a very barren field after the war, compared to the richness with which it flourished when I was a child. There were only two legitimate theatres (one of them boringly inaccessible—too far by public transport and too difficult to park by one's own) compared to the many of my youth. Now there is a vigorous stirring of Australian playwrights, and a crop of small playhouses and theatre clubs, but still the best of Australian talent leaves home. But forty or fifty years ago, we had Her Majesty's, the Criterion, the Theatre Royal, the Tivoli—we had whole visiting companies from England and America and opera companies from Italy—and my father had them all as patients. He was the official theatre doctor to all the companies, and so a great deal of my time was spent behind the wings, chasing through the corridors and dressing-rooms, while he was attending one of the company.

There was no discernible link between bridge games, death and drama; nevertheless, memories of one fade inevitably into memories of the other.

My mother's influence embedded in me the belief

that to play bad bridge was worse than boring; it bordered on a sin. It seemed easier never to learn. The bridge table would be set and ready by 11.30 a.m.—the bridge cloths, green baize or velour, bordered in gold-flecked brocade ribbon; the score pads with their four-cornered symbols of diamonds, hearts, clubs and spades; the freshly sharpened pencils still smelling of wood shavings; and the cook of the day busily cutting sandwiches in the kitchen. The players all wore hats, and even though these honorary 'aunts' bore no relationship other than parental friends, they were never addressed solely by their Christian names. At teatime I was allowed in to gaze at them, and once earned my mother's proud glance by a long, appraising look at one.

'Aunt Marjorie's very pretty, isn't she, Mummie.'

My mother, preening herself on her enchanting child, agreed.

'But I don't think much of the other two. Wherever did you get them from?'

The bridge table was a regular backdrop for these social comments, the supply of 'aunts' abundant. I once asked a new 'aunt' if she could remove her hat, the better to see her face, then let out a horrified cry to my mother, 'Oh no! Ask her to put it on again!'

I asked one lady sipping her tea if I could carefully watch her drink.

'Yes, darling, but why?'

'Because my daddy says you drink like a fish.'

My mother's bridge games were almost sacred events—to fall out without due warning an unforgiveably inconsiderate act, the more so if my father were the messenger.

He came home one night and announced to my mother that he had just been called to see a friend of hers, but that 'she didn't know much about it'.

My mother was a little shocked. 'Do you mean she was *drunk*?'

'Worse than that,' said my father. 'Dead.'

This really shocked her. 'She can't be dead—I'm playing bridge with her tomorrow.'

'Not tomorrow, dear.'

So, for me, death seemed the suitably dramatic end to any conversation, bringing with it no discomforting strangeness.

When there were no more family deaths to give colour to our days, my father's patients could always be relied upon.

They were all part of our lives, in those days of close family doctor and patient relationships. There were the Pierce boys, a family of rugged fishermen and keen amateur yachtsmen, whose favourite family joke was that my father had circumcised one of the younger boys 'crooked'. Twice a week my father drove to the fish market in the early morning and came home with a car load of fresh Pierce fish, a sack of oysters which I was taught to open at a very early age, and two or three live lobsters romping around in the back of the car and waving their antennae through the windows at startled passers-by. Every morning my father visited a rich and elderly bachelor friend to check his far from robust but nevertheless relatively stable health, except on the rare occasions when his housekeeper would telephone. 'Mr Cheek says, would the doctor mind not calling this morning as he is not feeling very well.'

We all mourned when one of his old ladies died, for she whiled away the last of her senile and bed-ridden days composing couplets to be recited at the doctor's visit. These fitted the ailment of the day. When her nightdress was lifted to bare her abdomen, she shrilled:

'Pull down my shirt,
I'm Fanny the Flirt.'

and for an abscessed breast brought forth:

'Isn't it a pity—
That I've got a titty.'

On mornings when I was not at school I frequently accompanied my father on his rounds, sometimes visiting the patient and sometimes waiting in the car outside. If he left me in a doubtful slum area, he always admonished me, 'Now, if anyone speaks to you, just make a noise like a five-year-old girl' or whatever age was appropriate at the time. When he emerged he would sometimes tell me about the case. I remember some of our family intimates only through their ailments which, if they were startling enough, my father could not resist recounting. Thus, one plump and coyly coquettish lady was embedded in my consciousness since a tick had 'crawled up her'. My father felt her charms were forever damned because, as he put it, 'when I got to the poor brute, it had died'.

Actually, for me, all Sydney was an extension of the security of the house. My days never had an even tenor, but always an assured one, and certain events brought their certain flavour.

Was there ever a threat to this security, I now wonder? Financial threat may have been there but never to be taken seriously. In the 1930s so-called 'society' women thought little of popping into the pawn shops with their jewellery. This particularly appealed to my mother, whose fiscal week was ruled by Saturday's betting results. Many a Thursday morning on Tony McGill's settling day she would borrow Juliet's sapphire and diamond ring (now on my finger) or one of her diamond, ruby and emerald butterflies, ostensibly to wear to a party, but in reality to appease Tony that night. After a few days, Juliet would become both curious and querulous and, dependent on the race results, my mother would either fling back her jewellery or plead another party.

In our urban life, my consciousness of the depression was an awareness of a wicked man called Jack Lang, bent, it seemed, on ruining all our lives. I do remember a sense of apprehension, almost fearful, attached to this man. But my only experience of actual financial concern was the occasion on which my parents made a pact to give up smoking—in order to pay for my school fees.

The pact lasted a week. My mother gave in first. This did not appear to affect my education and the school fees were never mentioned again.

Darker moments have been pushed away, into another dimension. Every now and then, a sound, a smell, a chink of light or darkness breaks the happy carapace of memory. Sitting downstairs in a two-up, two-down Surry Hills tenement I watched my father disappear up the narrow stairs with his worn, brown leather 'doctor's' bag, while from upstairs came screams—neither cries nor shouts, but piercing, wrenching, beseeching screams. When he came down again, the screams would have stopped. Someone else came with him—an elderly man or woman, talking in low voices. I knew that the screams came from a woman upstairs who had cancer. I knew that my father had, out of his leather bag, stopped the screams. I do not remember how I knew this, how my father had seen fit to introduce me to reality but all my life I have remembered—screams, cancer, horror, fear. It did not have the remote and curious connection of Uncle Ken's pneumonia and the bread and sugar. This death (for surely the woman was dying) belonged to the real world, more affecting—not one's uncle from my fairy tale (albeit sometimes a Grimm's fairy tale) world— but a creature *in extremis.*

Nevertheless the flavour of illness was an exciting one, not only the patients' illnesses, but my own. Then my mother swamped me with presents: I lay in feverish anticipation every time she left the house for she never went out, even for half an hour, without returning with armfuls of treasures. When my appendix came out a whole room of the hospital was hung by my mother in pink brocade, and every day a new lace or satin pillow cover arrived with a pillow spray of flowers in the appropriate colours, to pin beside my face.

My tonsils and adenoids came out in my father's surgery, suitably draped in sterile sheets, and I, aged four, was attended by three doctors. I am told that I sat up on the table as the anaesthetic wore off and lisped at them: 'You three damned doctors get to hell out of here.'

No recollections of luxury attend the occasion on which I swallowed a shilling: that was my mother's adventure. I was standing in a queue at the green-grocer's waiting to buy an ice-cream and, undecided as to flavour, was tapping my teeth reflectively with the shilling. In a flash it was gone: I flew home, thoroughly alarmed. The radiologist was a gambling crony of my mother's—as they waited for the X-ray of my innards to be developed, my mother laid bets with him on whether heads or tails would show. The shilling emerged side on.

Once I woke at night to an unfamiliar sound. Not the easy, raucous street sounds, but voices—measured and urgent—from the drawing-room. My grand-mother's and my father's voices raised, but, astound-ingly, mingled: no interpreter between them, and a lower voice, my grandfather's. The voices rose and fell but were definitely angry—a collective, barely con-trolled anger, quite different to the familiar sound of exasperation. When I had climbed out of bed and gone to investigate, the conference had broken up, my father pushing past, running down the stairs, my mother in her nightdress running after him. I knew he was leaving. She half fell down the stairs, her breasts escaping the nightdress, throwing herself at his legs and calling, 'Jim, Jim', before I was led back to bed by Nana. It seemed a long time later when my father came and sat by my bed to tell me he was going away. I cried, and clutched and begged. He promised he would not go. And for the first and only time I saw my father cry. To me it was a victory—but a victory that haunts me.

Soon after, my mother went to Melbourne for some weeks with Aunt Juliet. I now wonder whether this was a trial separation. For I remember a sense of something like shame—or dread?—attached to her absence. Children at school seemed to be aware of it, and wonderful presents, mostly jewellery, arrived for me every week. Also, about this time there was a visiting Englishman, called Geoff Seedley, high in the Heinz hierarchy, who gave me a string of seed pearls, to whom my father referred as 'your mother's fifty-seventh variety'. So, I expect that whatever drama may have erupted in their private lives was dissolved in laughter.

CHAPTER 4

About twice a week my father took me to see his mother. Grannie Richardson was a more remote figure than any in my mother's family. She had come to Australia as a young bride and when asked about my father's birth, was apt to say that the keel was laid in Ulster, but the ship launched in Australia. She had married twice and so earned the addition of the surname by which I always referred to her. This must also have denoted some extra mark of respect, for as I called my other grandmother 'Nana', there was no danger of confusion. Grannie Richardson was very beautiful, possessed of a wry humour, a cutting tongue, and a far less volatile temperament than those of my mother's side of the family among whom I lived. When she, who had little money, won first prize in the State Lottery—the then considerable sum of £5000—she did not tell her husband until the following day for fear of the possibility that he would keep her up all night talking about it. A further six months of weekly ticket buying with no additional profit incurred her disgust with the whole affair and the belief that it was in some way 'crooked'. Her first husband, my grandfather, died when my father was four. I have one photograph of him, and my father only ever told me one incident in his life—that single-handed and bare-fisted he fought, and presumably vanquished, for he lived to tell the tale, two of Ned Kelly's gang. Grannie Richardson, twice widowed in her fifties, ended her days in a small apartment near our house, glued to the wireless and immersed in a passion which, though born late in life, burned fiercely—she bet on the horses.

Even more than most Australians, I was brought up in an atmosphere where gambling in all forms, but especially horse-racing, was an important and integral part of our lives. Saturday evenings were the high spot of the week, for then Nana's drawing-room was full of racing friends of my grandfather's and from early morning when I was allowed to pick my winner with

a pin from the newspaper, until late at night, Saturdays were given over to racing talk. I once dreamt correctly a 20 to 1 winner: for three subsequent Friday nights I was sent to bed early with a glass of hot milk and a copy of the Form Guide under my pillow—but it was an isolated occasion and try as I would my importance as an oracle faded. Everyone who came in close contact with our household participated in this pursuit—friends, family, tradespeople, servants, and animals. Timmy Eakin, our talking budgerigar, whose first words were 'Doctor Eakin's surgery', soon added 'Thursday's Sporting Papers!' in the raucous call of the newsboy to his repertoire, and it was long accepted that Saturday night's dinner would be a very bleak and scrappy affair if Rosa Toomey, the cook, had had a 'bad day'.

Rosa was the doyenne of a succession of servants, all of startlingly eccentric character. Did our household attract these individuals, I wonder, or did it mould them to its own shape? Rosa Toomey came to my grandmother before my mother's marriage and remained for thirty-five years. Somewhere in the past,

My grandmother, father and grandfather Eakin (*c.* 1892), just before his death at thirty-one.

one presumed, was a Mr Toomey, for there was certainly a product of their union, but he was never mentioned, and Rosa's daughter and subsequent grandchildren were shadowy figures in her life which centred upon our house. As Rosa grew older her taciturnity increased and her appearance became ever stranger. When well over seventy, her hair was dyed regularly but not thoroughly, so that patches of silvery white and yellow-ochre showed with a clarity and reckless abandon through the reddish magenta of her choice. This mottling of hue may have been her hair's protesting reaction to the permanent waving to which it was subjected, at seven shillings and sixpence a time— once a month. Her devotion and loyalty to every member of my family was intense. She never, however, accepted Great-aunt Juliet as anything but an inter-loper and resented, verbally and loudly, her presence.

'Interfering old busybody,' she would mutter, flicking the duster viciously over the pile of bric-à-brac on the overcrowded dressing-table, while Juliet supervised operations from her pile of lace pillows. Aunt Juliet's readily summoned deafness came conveniently to the fore during these battles.

Grannie Richardson (Margaret Agnew), my paternal grandmother, aged sixteen.

'What did you say, Mrs Toomey?' (Juliet never called her Rosa.)

'Silly old cow!' Rosa bellowed back, shunting the broom between Juliet's feet.

But, deafness, real or assumed, being the most unanswerable of weapons, Rosa never emerged victorious from these encounters. And, as if in final surrender, she wept at Aunt Juliet's funeral.

I remember all our other servants with such vividness that it is hard to believe in the relative shortness of their stay with us—a duration necessitated by their numbers and variety in a span of twenty-five years. However briefly they remained, their personal dramas became a family concern. Amy was coloured, from one of the Pacific Islands, and we all listened in sympathy as she paced the flat roof, occasionally howling like a dog, every full moon.

Lily was eighteen, exceedingly pretty and unmistakably pregnant. One of eleven children, her already overburdened parents asked my father to intervene on behalf of her sailor suitor, father of the baby, who having agreed willingly to marry her, was mystified by her contemptuous refusal. To my father's enquiry of the reason for her reluctance, Lily answered: 'Because he's too short and he can't dance.'

And marry him she would not, so one more baby was added to her mother's brood.

Bina's only eccentricity was her insistence on wearing her starched white apron back to front: to keep it clean. She was certainly partial to a drink or two, but this passed without comment until she disappeared one weekend and was found in the adjacent Kings Cross cinema when the cleaners opened it on Monday morning. She had slipped happily between the seats at the late Saturday night showing.

When I was three I had as nurse the manservant of a friend of my father's, a judge on furlough from the Solomon Islands, who, having brought O'Kenny to Sydney with him, was at a loss how to occupy him. O'Kenny and I were happy in each other's company, but his authority came to an end when my parents discovered how we spent our days. I lay on my back under my father's car, catching on my tongue any stray drops of water or oil which fell from the running board while O'Kenny kept watch. Of this gentle creature I remember only two very large, bare, patient, coal-black feet.

Dougherty and Merle, who sounded like a music hall turn, were in fact mother and daughter of Irish extraction. Mr Dougherty had deserted Dougherty early in their married life and she suffered Merle ever after in a spirit of atonement for her mistake. We suffered her for the excellence of Dougherty's sweeping and polishing, for she was a vacant-minded and adenoidal girl who spent most of her day scurrying out of the way of her mother's vituperative tongue.

However, she won her permanent place in the honours list of family favourites by her impromptu greeting on the morning she found my parents sleeping on the floor. They shared, at the time, a large but shaky bed whose spring framework fitted imperfectly on the base. From time to time the inner part of the bed would go crashing to the floor, one side tilting crazily in the air. On this occasion, they had come home late from a party and it hardly seemed worth the trouble to haul it back to base. They settled down for the night as best they could on that part of the bed which rested levelly on the floor. Merle's startled cry awoke them over the tea-tray in the morning: 'Ooow! Whatever have yous two been up to?'

Nancy was in all practical ways the perfect servant. She was also rather alarmingly unbalanced, but this sober fact did not strike me until she came to work for me and my husband years after she had left my

mother's house. There, she was tolerated for her
eccentricities but joyously appreciated for what was an
undeniably keen, albeit macabre, sense of fun. There,
too, her pathologically intense likes and dislikes
were encouraged by my father for the amusement
he derived from their manifestations. One more than
normally frequent dropper-in at meal times would sit,
empty plate in front of her, while Nancy ostentatiously
served to the right and left, muttering in prim, clipped
Scottish accents as she passed behind her chair,
'Greedy bitch!' No amount of scolding by my mother
would force Nancy to desist and so, on the nights of
the poor woman's visits, my mother herself served at
table. Nancy had come out to Australia and to us from
the most rigorously trained English households and
she shed her inhibitions in our house with joy and
determination. Her behaviour remained ever meticu-
lous: it was the cruder forms of speech which gave her
particular delight. Passages and stairways rang with
Nancy's clear, pure voice pealing out the monosyllabic
obscenities she seemed just to have learnt.

'Ha, ha, ha—now isn't that a funny wee word,' we
heard over the hum of the Hoover in appreciation of
her newest acquisition.

I have to admit that in all probability she learnt

them in our house—if not from a member of the family, then from one of the tradesmen or various hangers-on or droppers-in for whom there was always a kettle boiling on the stove in readiness for a cup of tea. Four years after I had gone to live in England my mother died suddenly and I flew out to Australia to comfort my father. Nancy had long since gone home and a plump motherly Australian called Dulcie was in her place. I met Dulcie in tears one day.

'Oh, Mrs Dalton,' she wailed, 'that little bird just gave me such a turn! I could have sworn, dear, darling Mrs Eakin was still alive and in this room. As clear as anything, that little bird just said, "Oh, shit!"'

CHAPTER 5

J ust as some pervasive spirit of unconventionality seemed to grip all our servants, so, too, were our domestic livestock a memorable collection. My earliest recollection was of a large and rather fierce Australian galah. These are pure white cockatoos, with flaming pink crests, and ours hopped up and down in his cage, screeching angrily, and never succeeding in endearing himself to anyone. Samuel Pepys was the only dog I was ever allowed: for the four short years of his life, we never succeeded in house-training him, and we never broke him of his preference for my grandmother's hall carpet on which to deposit his mess. This caused furious rows, and when Pepys was finally run over, it was generally agreed that we could not risk a successor taking over his bad habits. So from then on, the house was invaded by a trio of exceedingly unusual cats. It had been my intention to have one cat, but shortly after acquiring a kitten named Roger (after one of the family friends), two more homeless kittens appeared in swift succession—one named Errol, after another friend, and the third Kiska, quite simply meaning 'cat' in Russian. These three castrated males quickly developed a most complex game, involving perfect timing and teamwork, with which they amused or startled any six o'clock guests, according to whether or not they were regular visitors. They lay low for a couple of hours before six, gathering strength no doubt for their performance, and then with an instinct for time never more than ten minutes out either way, they would come hurtling down the hall, claws and paws scratching on the parquet floor and—first Roger, then Errol, then Kiska—tear twice round the sitting-room floor, beneath and between feet, at furious pace, and finally launch themselves in formation on the window curtains. Straight up one side of the curtains they shot, across the pelmet, and straight down the other side. Round the room once more, and out.

Unhappily, they were too decorative and frivolous a trio to be any check on the rats which were our next companions. The back door of our house led onto a dirty cul-de-sac, littered with garbage and the decaying fences of older houses than ours. Next door was the back entrance of a restaurant of always suspect cleanliness, and of obviously unsanitary antiquity. I suppose the rats had lived a life of luxury there for years for, when it was suddenly demolished, the indignation and deprivation shone transparently out of their furious eyes as they glared at us in the dark. They literally swarmed into our house, to the extent that I awoke one night to find one perched, fixing me with baffled and reproachful stare, on the end of my bed. This happening finally prodded my father into action: hitherto he had tended to regard the visitors with indulgent amusement and to the female complaints around him was apt to reply, with something like nostalgia, that he'd been accustomed to rats dropping onto his sleeping face when he was in the Navy. But now he turned our problem over to a firm of pest and rodent exterminators called Fletcher & Hawks and, in exchange for a substantial cheque, settled back in preparation for peace.

Various representatives of Fletcher & Hawks appeared, dived into manholes, cracks and crevasses, flirted with the rats, and disappeared again. The rats'

eyes grew angrier and more reproachful, but they
rallied and it seemed that their ranks closed into
something more like formation tactics. Various key
personnel took up permanent posts around the house,
so that one could almost be certain of meeting a
particular rat at a particular time and place. My father
passed this information on to Fletcher & Hawks; more
money changed hands, and more white-coated men
appeared. More rats also appeared, and the din around
our dustbins at night was now impossible to ignore.
One had to walk down a narrow passageway past
the dustbins in order to reach the garage, so that
this became an occasion for apologetic explanation
whenever a guest was winded in passing by a disturbed
rat. Short of asking the Fletcher & Hawks staff to
come and live with us awhile to observe our condition,
my father, by now exasperated, could get neither
satisfaction nor his money back, and now in possession
of a handsome fee, they were inclined to by-pass his
letters as hysterical exaggeration.

He composed what proved to be his final letter
with some care and enjoyment. Presuming that there
were indeed a Mr Fletcher and a Mr Hawks, he
addressed his letter to them personally and, after
setting out in detail the lengths to which he had gone

to provoke satisfactory action, and the remuneration they had received for their services, he asked that their efforts be redoubled. But, he added, it would be with some sense of loss that he would witness the passing from his life of his now two most familiar companions: one, an active and industrious rat who lived in the floor boards under his desk, and whose chirpings and burrowings accompanied his working hours and lightened the clinical quiet of his surgery; the other, a large and friendly rat who nightly lay in wait behind the dustbin lid, and as he walked to his car, came hurtling forth in response to the merest flicking of his fingers and to whom he hoped he might still have time to teach a few tricks. In view of their long association and of the way these two had flourished under their patronage and care, he had taken the liberty of naming them respectively, Fletcher and Hawks. By these names were these two mildly notorious rodents becoming known to the inhabitants of the 'Cross' and to his large circle of patients.

The following week Mr Fletcher and Mr Hawks arrived in person, and within a few days the ranks of the rats dwindled and faltered, and soon they had all disappeared.

CHAPTER 6

My grandfather was a quiet and saintly man, whose presence in this matriarchal house was nevertheless some restraining influence on the family dramas. He and I had an especially close relationship: I called him 'Sammie' and he treated me as his friend and equal. From the time I could walk, I accompanied him on his early morning swim, which performed the triple function of getting me out of the house, teaching me to swim, and establishing an affinity with my grandfather and his family.

Every morning at 6 a.m. we walked through the empty streets and the grimy park, known as the Domain, where tramps were just stirring under their newspapers, to the fenced-in enclosure at the harbour's edge, the Domain Baths. The Baths were in the same tongue of the harbour as the docks and I shudder to think of the oil and refuse in which I must have wallowed and flourished. Until I was four we went to the Men's Baths, and when I was nearly two I graduated from Sammie's back to a sturdy dog-paddle of my own. The men swam naked, so that at four it was decided that I was too old to share their morning freedom and my grandfather dropped me off alone at the Ladies' Baths next door. We went every morning, summer and winter, in rain or sun; and, walking home, Sammie and I would play the Shakespeare Game. Every day I had to say one reasonably well-known line from one of Shakespeare's plays or sonnets, and Sammie took up the quotation from there, reciting until I told him to stop.

We walked to his mother's house for breakfast—he had breakfasted with her every morning of his married life, and for me it was yet another household of which I felt myself to be an integral part. My great-grandmother was a wiry, bird-like, little creature, who died, almost on her feet (having just cooked the breakfast) at the age of ninety-nine. Aunt Emma and Uncle Charles and Harry lived with her. Harry was my grandfather's youngest brother, and was never called

'Uncle' because he was 'simple' and about the same mental age as myself. He teased me all through breakfast and I loathed him. Uncle Charles suffered from terrible asthma and had never been able to do much, and Aunt Emma had never married, so my grandfather supported them all.

I think I was fond of my great-grandmother, although I felt the lack in Charles and Emma and Harry of the soft yet strident, rich and enveloping warmth of my grandmother's environment. There I heard no wonderful stories, nor lay on lace pillows being tickled, nor was tempted hourly to some titbit of highly unsuitable and indigestible food. My great-grandmother was born in Australia and so her parents must have been some of the earliest settlers. I learnt nothing of her background, and everyone whom I might now ask is dead. What tales Nana's imagination could have weaved from her material!

The house was a kindly, but silent one—in itself, to me, a strange and intimidating setting. I expect I resented this what, to one brought up in my grandmother's aura, must have appeared perplexing chill. My grandmother and Juliet were a gushing fount of loudly expressed affection and solace. Whatever the ill, be it physical, mental or emotional, there was on hand a quickly proffered remedy—a laugh to heal a wound, a cheque to fill a financial chasm, the two words 'Never mind' the most oft-repeated and often heeded ones of my childhood. Charles, in adulthood recognised as the gentlest and dearest of creatures, seemed a crabby and alien soul to my small, spoilt and affection-pampered self.

Once I was very ill with gastro-enteritis (brought on, one now wonders, by Nana's unholy feasts). On my first visit to Great Grannie after the crisis had passed, I sat, wan and thin, staring ahead—my eyes, said my great-grandmother, 'like those of a little angel huge in her dear, thin, little face'. Great Grannie wondered if, close to death as I had been, some intimations of immortality lingered about my thoughts; so ethereal, she said, was my expression.

'Tell me, darling, what are you thinking?'

'Well,' lisped the little angel, 'I've got a mouthful of thpit and I wath just wondering which one of you three old things to give it to.'

I was ten when Great Grannie died and Sammie and I no longer had our early mornings together. Instead of the Ladies' Baths I went to the surf at Bondi Beach with my father and Sammie breakfasted at home.

After his death (peaceful and abrupt), no masculine voice was raised to prevent the family dramas, which now raged unabated. My father's voice was raised only too frequently to my mother, but this was unhappily no remedy, as he had access to only one side of the contestants, and nobody now existed, as had my grandfather, to stop Juliet egging my grandmother on. Out of loyalty to my mother and in deference to her husband's wishes, my grandmother had never again spoken to her sisters since my mother's marriage, but she still loved her family dearly and as soon as my grandfather was dead, Juliet tried to heal the breach. I, who had never heard them spoken of except in terms of derision, now began to hear their virtues and talents extolled. Nana now paid an occasional visit to them, and on her return regaled me with delightfully irrelevant details of their lives.

'They are four wonderful women,' she said. 'They never do any visiting excepting to specialists—and an occasional X-ray man.'

As always, physical handicaps came into the picture and from them I started to form incongruous pictures

---

(*left*) Me, aged four, with Great-aunt Emma in the garden and (*right*) with Great Grannie.

of my octogenarian great-aunts. After one visit she informed me: 'One sister has an intestinal rupture on the heart side, of late development. She is a great swimmer and always dives off the board with a double somersault. That is the only way the doctors think she might have developed it.'

I struggled to accept the likelihood of this story for, although I could not suddenly feel affection or affinity with these unknown relations, I was intrigued at the possibility of having a great-aunt who could perform such a feat.

About this time, their beloved brother, Spot, who had also never married, became seriously ill. All the sisters were growing more frail, and especially Netta, the heroine of the high dive. Netta's special self-imposed task was preparing the one solid food that Spot was taking, which was generally supposed to be his last relinquished carnal pleasure: bread and butter cut wafer-thin—thin, as was the family boast, as only Netta could cut it. Every day Netta dragged herself down to the kitchen, sliced the bread ever thinner and thinner, and sat by Spot's bedside feeding him the morsels. One day, the stairs up and down to the kitchen proved too much for Netta—poor Spot had to go without his treat, as no-one else could be trusted to match Netta's lightness of touch. My grandmother was sitting by his bed when he beckoned her close and hissed in her ear.

'Dora—Dora—would you do something for me?'

'Of course, Spot darling, what would you like?'

'Oh, Dora, if only I could have a really *thick* piece of bread and butter I think I would feel better!'

Now that the two old ladies, my grandmother and great-aunt, were alone, Juliet still retained her purple bedroom, but she slept downstairs in my grandmother's bedroom. There they lay, twin-bedded and, in Juliet's case, as often as not, befurred, receiving friends and seldom, as they grew older, rising. They slept for long periods of the day, and at night they awoke and flourished. No food was too rich or too highly spiced for their digestions and throughout the night my mother ran up and down the stairs from her kitchen to their bedroom preparing whatever dish they fancied. About dawn, the two old ladies, refreshed and replete, would drop into a deep sleep and my mother would crawl upstairs, exhausted, to her bed. Often during the night a wordy battle would have raged: this tired my mother and stimulated Nana and Juliet. But my mother never learnt to ignore them in the mornings, and could never resist going down for their breakfast order which, whatever their gastronomic indulgences of the previous night, was invariably hearty. One morning Aunt Juliet, still smarting from some insult of the night's fray, sulked and reluctantly joined in her hunger strike by my grandmother, refused breakfast for them both. My mother was determined to rise above such pettiness: upstairs in our kitchen I watched her slamming butter on toast, eggs on bacon, marmalade in its silver dish, coffee and milk in Juliet's heavy Victorian silver jugs, muttering with irritation as she manipulated the lot onto the massive silver tray and angled her way with it down the twisting narrow stairs.

'Here's your breakfast, girls,' she called from the door, with an attempt at gaiety.

'I told you, Lyndall,' snapped Juliet, while rising, nevertheless and settling herself expectantly on her pillows, 'that we didn't want any breakfast.'

'Well,' said my mother, 'in that case, you bloody well needn't *have* any breakfast!' and, marching to the window, with one mighty heave, she hurled the loaded tray out into the street.

My mother suffered agonies of remorse from these outbreaks but, what with lack of sleep, lack of privacy, and constant provocation, her nerves could never weather another encounter for long. Of course, I missed a great deal of the fun when I was at school and so the few occasions when my mother literally let fly were to me gloriously explosive highlights in a situation continually smouldering with tension.

CHAPTER 7

My mother loved flowers passionately and as we had no garden her passion found expression in arranging brimming bowls in every room. These she did exquisitely, with care and devotion, but was seldom allowed to indulge in her artistry alone. Once all the vases in the sitting-room had been filled with water and wire and the flowers freed from their wrapping, my grandmother would come in and take up her seat. On top of the chimney-piece was a deep, heavy earthenware trough, and this was always a challenge to my mother's skill: the flowers had to be just the right length and just the right weight to balance in their wire cage. One day my grandmother was watching this intricate task and after my mother had placed each flower in its place she, talking the while, would skip forward and give the whole erection a tweak. Tight-lipped but restrained, my mother persevered, and my grandmother continued to pull a flower here and push a flower there each time she turned to the table for the next one. Finally when the whole pattern was almost complete, my grandmother pulled a flower just a shade too hard and slowly the wire cage tipped forward—the work of half-an-hour lying forlornly horizontal. 'Aaaah!' bellowed my mother, with a terrible cry of release: she grasped the heavy trough tightly at either end, and with all the force she could summon threw it intact to the ceiling. There was a splendid crash: a cascade of water, wire, flowers, pieces of pottery shot all over the room and my grandmother, seriously alarmed, went pale with fright.

'Lyndall,' she whispered, 'I think you've gone mad!'

This was an unexpected bonus in weapons and my mother seized upon it. She whirled upon my grandmother, wild-eyed.

'That's it,' she shrieked, 'I am! I am!'

Battering on the wall with her fists, she raised her eyes to the dripping ceiling, 'Mad! Mad! Mad!'

My grandmother scurried downstairs as fast as she could, and my mother was left to regain her composure and mop up the debris in peace.

Many of the rows were precipitated by Aunt Juliet. She was an extremely stupid woman, although, in a childish way, sometimes endearingly so. Uncle Harry had fallen through our floor a rich man, but had left his money so tied up by trusts that his silly widow had little opportunity to dissipate it, as she undoubtedly would have done. One of her few financial freedoms was a charge account at Sydney's best department store, David Jones, which was paid monthly by the trustees. This was a recognised family preserve or, I should say, recognised by Aunt Juliet in moments of generosity or bribery and by my mother perpetually. When Aunt Juliet wished to make amends for some act of idiocy, she would tell my mother to go and buy herself something 'on my account at David Jones'. On the other hand, whenever my mother wanted to buy something, usually for me, which she could not afford (and as the week's housekeeping would invariably

---

Nana and my mother. A street photographer has caught them both without gloves. But this was war-time and, judging by the fan, a hot day.

have been eaten up or gone into Tony McGill's pocket, she could rarely afford it), she would say with a comforting and conspiratorial air, 'Come along. We'll put it on Aunt Juliet's account, at David Jones.' We had wonderful shopping sprees on Aunt Juliet's account, and terrible rows each month when the bill came in. Quite often, my mother bought Aunt Juliet something even more expensive to pacify her: this went on the following month's account, and so we had four clear weeks for the effect of the 'gift' to wear off. My mother's attitude to money was delightful, but impractical. She had been brought up by my grandmother in the same way as I was, and by having repeated to her frequently the words of my great-grandfather who was reputed to have dinned into the ears of his twelve children, 'Never worry about money. It's only an attitude of mind, and the next best thing to being very rich is to think you're very rich.'

As he was, in fact, very rich, this philosophy didn't have such disastrous effects as it was to have on the lives of his descendants, who had managed in following his principles to get through most of his money.

Great-aunt Juliet, doubtless on her way home from David Jones in the 1930s.

My grandmother was untiring in her efforts (in my mother's case entirely successful) to teach disrespect and contempt for money. She carried this to the length of refusing to write the word, and later in her letters to me, usually enclosing a cheque, would refer to it as 'Filthy L—'. It was, indeed, to her a dirty word.

In consequence, my mother, who was not very rich, was constantly in debt. She never really grasped the principle of accounting, but she did know that bills were almost invariably typewritten, and that a typewritten envelope was apt to contain a bill. So she evolved the happy plan of putting all typewritten envelopes unopened in the kitchen drawer. There they lay, piling up explosive potential until the day the drawer would no longer close and various apologetic little men would present themselves at my father's door. He, poor man, invariably paid, and so there would be another unholy row. Many years of marriage never taught him the futility of trying to instil into his family his own thrifty and practical principles. We were hopelessly lost to my grandmother's far gayer and pleasanter pattern for living.

My father's only financial indulgence was in racing, and he was constantly working out a 'system'. Very occasionally the system worked and my father smugly came home with bulging pockets. On these occasions my mother attempted to have him make up her own losings, with no success.

Once, after a fairly spectacular win and a firm refusal to my mother's entreaties, he went off to Richard Hunt's, Sydney's best men's shop, and bought himself several pairs of imported, expensive and superfluous woollen socks. My mother, on seeing the socks, was incensed.

'Amy,' she called to the maid, 'Come here and catch me a moth!'

Apart from racing, I don't know if there was anything peculiarly Australian about our home life. Perhaps the informality and wholehearted participation of all friends and attendants in our family affairs would have been impossible in a stricter culture. Sydney is a big city, but to some extent it still remains true that everybody knows their neighbour's business, just as in a small country town anywhere in the world. I used to run away (certainly not because I was unhappy but for the fun of the journey) about once a month, but nobody worried. Usually I ended up in the greengrocer's (Greek) at one end of the street, or in the tobacconist's kiosk at the other, serving behind the counter. This was to me the ultimate adventure: all the shopkeepers in the Cross knew me and were quite willing to humour me, and my parents were fairly certain where to find me at bedtime. This was in an area quite as urban and crowded as present-day Knightsbridge, and so to a certain extent a spirit of frontier-day friendliness must have survived.

Everyone, of course, knew my father. His vast practice embraced all of the Cross and its inhabitants on the fringes of the underworld: the docks of Woolloomooloo; the slums of Surry Hills; and beyond them into the fashionable purlieus of the eastern suburbs. The traffic policeman on duty held up even the trams for him, and he was friend and counsellor to all the prostitutes of the Dirty Half Mile. He normally remained teetotal all year until my birthday three days before Christmas, when he drank, fairly solidly, until New Year's Day. On Christmas Day he visited his poorest patients, taking them presents—a bottle of beer, wrapped in newspaper tied with a blue bow; a basket of a piece of soap, an orange and a bottle of eau-de-cologne with a pink bow—and stayed to chat and often have a drink with them. If it was beer, or gin or whisky (which he usually would have taken them) he would arrive home with a merry, tipsy chuckle and if it was a particularly revolting glass of cheap port and a wedge of rock-hard Christmas cake, he would surreptitiously deposit these in the earth of the pot plant usually gracing the 'parlour'. Sometimes he brought home stories which had particularly amused him, and he loved the colourful vernacular of his slum patients—such as the usual East Sydney way of expressing righteous surprise at an unmarried pregnancy—'I was only out with 'im once and 'e nicked it orf me.' Sometimes stories of his own rejoinders reached us, such as his encounter at the fashionable and respectable ladies club, the Queens Club. At this stronghold of virtuous matrons a notice, redundant one would have thought, was posted on the board to the effect that males were not permitted above the first floor.

One morning at 7.30 a.m. my father was walking downstairs following an emergency visit to a patient on the second floor when he was greeted with horrified surprise by a member in dressing-gown and curlers.

'Why, Doctor Eakin! Whatever are you doing here at this hour?'

'Sssh,' said my father. 'I overslept!'

His red doctor's light burned above our front door all night and the doorbell rang through the nights almost as often as the telephone. One particularly busy night—a baby having been delivered, the wounds of a gang fight stitched up, and the usual drunk dispatched home—my father fell into bed about 3 a.m., saying he would not be disturbed again for any emergency. Within ten minutes the doorbell rang. He cursed and snorted and turned over: nobody answered it and it went on pealing shrilly into the night. Whoever was ringing it was more determined than my father: eventually he was goaded out from under the bed-clothes. He stuck his head out of his window directly over the front door and bellowed a string of curses at his tormentor. It was Joe, the hot dog man from the mobile all-night stand on the corner. Joe was a small, timid man, but he stood his ground and when my father's invective had ceased, he blurted apologetically.

'I'm awful sorry, doctor, but your house is on fire.'

Actually it was the chimney of the house next door but the sparks were sufficient to get us all from our beds and my mother up on to the roof with the firemen who were then called. Joe came in for a cup of tea and it all ended as a hilarious tea party.

It is the laughter I remember and miss most poig-nantly. The rows and the laughter were daily doses on which we thrived: frequently the laughter arose out of the rows, or out of the tears which followed them. I remember seeing my mother in tears one day following an outburst of my father's and, puzzled by this constant drama in our lives, I asked her why she stood it. It seemed to me a one-sided persecution, as he never cried, and the kitchen drawer full of bills and the house full of interfering old ladies would never have occurred to me as a provocation.

'Well,' she sobbed, 'I *couldn't* live with the bastard if he didn't make me laugh so much.'

I think it was the clash and mingling of the Irish and Jewish temperaments which produced this climate of high dramatic comedy. The fact that the doors were open and everybody joined in was pure Australian.

CHAPTER 8

Although my father appeared in the role of resigned provider to a household of permanent guests, I think his enjoyment of their continual company equalled, in his much quieter way, my mother's. At least he could escape, and frequently did—not far, to be sure, for to reach his bed he had to undress in one room and make his way in striped pyjamas through the crowded sitting-room to the verandah where he slept. But he had no inhibitions about doing this and the evening's conversation continued to the accompaniment of his ferocious snores. He became, at this time, quite an established 'club man' and keen billiards player. His championship status ended on the day he shot himself; ever after, he found it painful and difficult to bend the affected knee into the prescribed position.

Actually his first two adventures with firearms weren't too serious: only on the third occasion was any bodily damage done. The pistol was of very small, very smart Spanish manufacture—just large enough to lie in the palm of his hand, and affording a more comforting and solid feel than the thin jingle of key rings or the like with which some men fidget. He first came to carry one of these on the advice of the police, who were concerned over his lone night calls into the underworld areas of dock and slum land. Sydney had during the thirties a crime wave of serious proportions, terrorised by a gang of slashers known as the Razor Gang, and it was against the possibility of attack by these assailants that the gun was bought. On his first day home with his new toy, my father indulged in a little quiet target practice in the surgery, but beyond a ricocheting bullet which gouged some plaster out of the surgery wall, splintered a glass case full of instruments and bounced harmlessly out into the light area, no untoward incidents occurred. Secure in the assumption that he now knew when it was liable to go off, and when it was not, he took the gun out with him at night for as long as the situation lasted, and occasionally fondled it by day as it lay in his desk drawer. When war broke out, all licences to own firearms were reviewed: my father took his pistol up to No. 3 Police Station where, over a cup of tea with the Station boys, he missed the sergeant's leg by inches.

On the afternoon he finally shot himself, my mother was upstairs and as usual entertaining some friends to tea. It was a humid, somnolent day, enervating; and the patient who was sitting by my father's desk cataloguing her woes was one of his regular and more boring hypochondriacs, whose long list of ailments needed no further response than an occasional murmur of sympathy. While making these reassuring noises, he idly fingered the pistol in the middle drawer of his desk, lying in its accustomed nest of old papers, tobacco pouches, and pipe cleaners. As usual it was loaded and, as usual, my father hadn't quite got the hang of it.

'I get these terrifying palpitations, Doctor— sometimes when I lie down I think I'm going to choke. And then, suddenly, I'll get a feeling of something awful about to happen—it's my nerves, I suppose. Don't you think I should have something to calm my nerves?'

'Mmmm,' said my father, and pulled the trigger.

The bullet made a deafening report, in the doubly confined space of the drawer, and of the consulting room. The initial impact of the drawer-bottom probably lightened the blow, which nevertheless neatly blew off part of my father's kneecap. The patient swooned—my father cursed and bellowed—the nurse ran in, first to mop up the blood and call an ambulance into which she assisted my father; then, to revive the patient and put her in a taxi. Upstairs my mother's guests exclaimed at the noise, but my mother assured them, 'Don't worry. The doctor's probably shot himself.'

It was not until some hours later that she learnt that her husband was in hospital, where he stayed for two weeks, the central figure of a good deal of amused attention.

Later that night, I opened the door to two plain-clothes policemen.

'Miss Eakin,' they said, 'you can tell that father of yours that if he doesn't learn to use that gun properly soon, we're going to take it away from him.'

While he was in hospital, the patient who had witnessed the accident recovered sufficiently to ring him for further professional advice. In fact, the hospital switchboard operators were pestered by the wretched woman, and finally agreed to ask the doctor for his opinion. The Sister on duty came one day, 'Mrs So-and-so is on the telephone. She says to tell you she has that sinking feeling again, and please, what should she do?'

'Tell her,' said my father, 'to strike out for the shore.'

CHAPTER 9

When I was thirteen, the tottering finances of the one remaining Miss Cheriton finally collapsed and Doone terminated its brief but illustrious ten years' existence. It had, as a school, made its mark: it had panache—it was smart—it provided good educational facilities, and its older pupils of the finishing school level had become locally renowned for their looks. The Doone girls, in the Sydney of that day, was a collective term conjuring up an image of youthful, well-educated beauty gathered for the picking under one roof and the eager and not too strict chaperonage of 'Cherry'. They frisked through amateur theatricals and the Arts, Government House dances, A.D.C.s, and the last of Cherry's money.

When the end came, I was enrolled in the most exclusive and expensive boarding-school in the state, Frensham. My memories of Frensham are all pleasant ones: experiences to shock and distress me may have occurred during those significant adolescent years, although by now, I was fairly shockproof, but I cannot recall them. My time at Frensham was one of deepening and happy expectancy of the future. Situated eighty miles from Sydney, the school buildings had grown gradually and were scattered through acres of beautiful mountain bushland. The mistresses, in those days, had all travelled out from England and with them they brought English educational ideas and principles, tempered and tailored to the Australian life and the Australian material on which they had to work. I doubt if many of them had had experience of the Australian father, and nothing to equip them for their encounters with mine. On the whole, however, I managed to preserve the illusion of a suitably paternal figure in my background, at the risk, on one occasion, of severe punishment.

The occasion was a school concert—not an official affair, but one produced entirely by the girls, which was traditionally known as a 'Scratch' concert. My musical background has produced no stirring of talent

in me. Although listening to music is one of my
greatest joys, I can play no instrument, nor recognise
by ear one note, and if ever I am obliged to sing,
nothing will emerge from my willing throat but a
painfully unmelodious dirge. I cannot remember what
paucity of numbers—it cannot have been talent—
caused me to be chosen as one of a chorus of four or
five girls to chant the Volga Boat Song. I suppose
some long-suppressed wish to be recognised as not
entirely unmusical led me, foolishly, to disclose the
fact in my weekly letter home. The Saturday morning
of the concert, I was in a state of happy and fairly
confident tension. As we were a country school,
served by a small local telephone exchange, telegrams
were telephoned through by the operator to the
Mistress on Duty, who was, on this day, the most
elderly, fussily eccentric and hysterically inclined
member of the staff. She sent for me at 10 a.m.:
the operator had telephoned through a telegram
addressed to me, for which Miss Livingstone
demanded adequate explanation. Written in Miss
Livingstone's elegant and flowing script, it read:
'Knock 'Em Rotten, Kid. Bing Crosby.'

Only my father could have sent it, and those that
followed at half-hourly intervals throughout the day.

I prayed, as I floundered for explanation and Miss Livingstone's hysteria mounted, that each one would be the last. But there seemed no end to my father's flow of invention that day. As each fresh summons to her room came, I listened to Miss Livingstone calling for first my form mistress, and then my house mistress and as she read out the latest horror, I watched the telephone with apprehension waiting for its next shrill attack. 'With you in Spirit' signed 'Nellie Melba' and, tersely, 'I hate you. Grace Moore.' From Australia's leading theatrical firm, J. C. Williamson's, came the entreaty, 'Is £150 a week enough?'

'Who is this man? I demand to know,' shrieked Miss Livingstone, waving at me the message 'We WANT you. M.G.M.' When I failed to answer this too, the council of my three inquisitors decided that the time had come to report the matter to the headmistress. The girl on the exchange had by now entered into the spirit of my father's intentions and was giggling so uncontrollably that she had even greater difficulty than usual in transmitting the messages to Miss Livingtone, who was, under the most sedate of circumstances, in a fairly advanced condition of deafness. This further indignity to the school was reported to Miss West, along with the sheaf

of offensive messages. As I refused, professedly
through ignorance, to divulge the name of the sender,
Miss West sighed, 'Very well—as you will not tell us
whom you believe to be sending these frivolous and
insulting messages, there is only one course you leave
open to me. I am very sorry to have to do this, but I
am afraid I shall be obliged to turn this entire matter
over to your father and he must deal with you as he
sees best.'

I escaped with no sterner punishment than being
deprived of my only chance of musical performance,
and without having 'owned up'. Neither did my
father.

CHAPTER 10

A large percentage of the girls were country bred, for Australians are not entirely conditioned to the boarding-school idea, and the majority of children who live in the cities attend day school. So many of the fathers were graziers—sheep and cattle breeders. I spent several of my school holidays with a particular friend whose father owned a sheep station, and who, like most country folk, came to Sydney only for the Easter Agricultural Show, the ram sales, and the two major social events of the Sydney calendar—the spring and autumn race meetings. He was a delightful man, tough, wry, and unpretentious, with a typically Australian humour and a typically Australian capacity for alcohol. One race day my mother met him, dressed in his city best, leaning against the entrance of the Members Stand of the Australian Jockey Club, the exclusive institution of which he was a member, hacking away at his upper dentures with a pen knife.

'Bloody things don't fit,' he complained. 'New this morning. Suppose I'll get 'em whittled down to shape before the last race.'

When the bush folk aren't racing in the cities they have their own local meetings—the Picnic Races, and a rollicking picnic they are, for the whole boisterous, drunken, hilarious week. The horses are either local nags, mounted by their owners, or they travel from country town to town, within a limited radius. The tracks are the best available field: the bookies are, on the whole, so crooked that it's wise to watch the race with one eye and your bookie with the other in case he beats a hasty retreat. The Picnic refers officially to the luncheon hampers brought by the spectators. Graziers for miles around are full up with house guests for their local Race Week; cocktail parties are held nightly at stations within a hundred mile radius, and it all culminates in the Picnic Race Ball, in somebody's wool shed. The local pub is always bursting with stretchers in the corridors and whisky and milk tends to be mixed with the standard Australian breakfast of steak and eggs.

The Australian homestead, for the most part, is a comfortable bungalow surrounded on all sides by a wide, covered, and wire-netted verandah, well stocked with liquor, occasionally air-conditioned, and usually lacking in any domestic staff beyond the wife of one of the men, who might condescend to come in mornings and do the 'rough'. Now, the grazier gets around in a Jeep or his private plane: when I was a child we rode from place to place, and horses were for use. We didn't think of getting dressed up to 'go riding'.

Summer holidays I stayed with a friend whose family had a boat at Palm Beach or, some years, we rented a house ourselves. For the six or seven weeks over Christmas, most of our friends moved down the coast, twenty-five miles or so, to one of the glorious palm-fringed northern beaches—Palm Beach, Whale Beach, Newport, Collaroy. At our seaside cottage one Christmas, the house party was kept awake for two nights by the deafening snores of a guest who left on the third day, profuse in thanks and apologies that he had driven the other occupant of his bedroom onto the verandah. Polite and indulgent laughter followed him down the path. When the last farewell had been waved at his vanishing motor car, my mother asked my father: 'Who was that, darling? A nice man, I thought.'

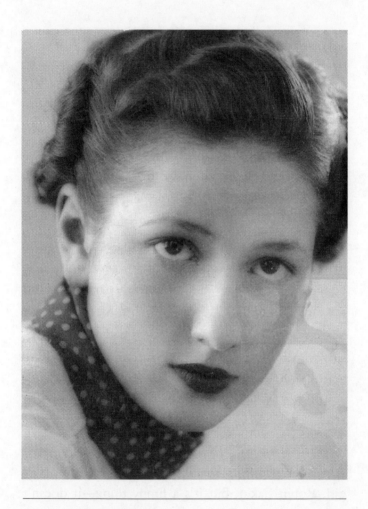

Me, aged about seventeen.

'Well, *I* don't know,' said my father crossly. 'Never seen him before in my life. Thought he was a friend of *yours.*'

At this particular house, my mother's hospitality had far outstripped the physical facilities of what was intended as a small family holiday cottage. A tent was erected in the back garden for myself and my friends: my mother usually spent the night on a swing hammock on the front porch, surrounded by those guests, laid out on divans and stretchers, whom she had been unable to squeeze into bedrooms. The liquor bill for the first month was so astronomical and my father's nights so disturbed that on this occasion he rebelled and one morning stormed up to town, snapping at my mother that, in future, she could have her 'bloody shooting box' to herself.

When I, in my teens, began to have an active and independent social life of my own I found that the life of our household struck some of my young escorts as unusual. One was reported to me as having said, 'Nice girl, Robin Eakin, but it's a funny thing—it doesn't matter what time of night you take her home, there always seems to be a strange man having a bath in that

Nana and me shopping in the late 1930s.

house.' Another bewildered young man, whom I had
not thought to introduce to my father, made enquiries
around town as to the identity of the big man in
striped pyjamas who wandered about the house. This
didn't bother me: what really plagued my adolescence
was the nightly tussle of trying to round the bend in
the stairs and the short stretch of corridor to the front
door without having my beau of the evening waylaid
by my grandmother and great-aunt. Every night they
hovered at their bedroom door at the foot of the stairs
and so finely judged was their timing that invariably
their two heads popped round the door and hailed me
just as I reached the angle of stair and hall. Neither
affection nor good manners would have halted me,
even had it meant, as it frequently did, pushing one or
both of them aside; but they were cunning enough to
direct their attentions on to the young man who,
blushing furiously, must give full account of his
antecedents, occupation and, if feasible, intentions.

Even more shaming to me were their frequent
sorties into Sydney's night-life. Now the city abounds

We dressed up for charity events just before and during the
Second World War. (*above*) I was the ringmaster at a
Glamour Circus, and (*below*) the leader of a conga line for
yet another 'good cause'.

in restaurants and nightclubs, but then there were only two really smart ones, Romano's and Prince's, and it was in one of these two that I spent almost every evening. At least once a week, Nana and Juliet rose from their beds, dressed as for a ball, reserved a floor table and sat watching me dance round the floor with my embarrassed escort. The head waiters adored them, for they ate prodigiously, drank quantities of champagne, and the society photographers flocked to take their picture. This would appear next day, to my rage and chagrin, beaming over the champagne bucket from the society pages, captioned 'Robin Eakin's grandmother and great-aunt'.

We, in our teens, led a more sophisticated life than English or European adolescents: freer, and at the same time, simpler. We lived in or on the sea all summer, danced half the night, and raced our parents' cars up and down the perilous coastal roads. These were the years just before the war and we were conscious of nothing but the sun, and the sea, and the wide, warm, free country spilling its splendours about us.

Joan McGrath (now Platt-Hepworth) and me supporting the Red Cross in Martin Place during the war.

CHAPTER 11

When war came to Sydney I had the measles. I remember Nana woke me up to announce the news and insisted on cracking a bottle of champagne by my bedside—not in celebration, but as her means of greeting any crisis. My mother found her natural element. Although Sydney was a front-line Pacific base for supply and recreational purposes, the only real danger that threatened the thousands of U.S. service-men who spent part of their war fighting the Battle of Sydney was that of overfeeding by my mother. She gladly filled the emotional vacuum left by their American 'moms', but this was as nothing compared

The war! Americans galore ...

to the zest with which she shovelled food into the stomachs of the troops. Almost nightly I lost an admirer to the attractions of our kitchen. Eventually she took to feeding whole squadrons stationed in New Guinea as one base-returning pilot after another went back laden with hampers for those of her 'boys' already back in the jungle. My father, too, played his part with relish. He was made Chief Medical Officer for the Port of Sydney, and supervised the supply, staffing and training of a chain of underground medical posts around the docks. His working kit was a tin helmet and boiler suit, and although the biggest size available, its fly and stomach buttons refused to meet, and so he went repeatedly to action stations in a seemingly suitable state of emergency. The alert blast on the air-raid sirens was the signal for action stations for our entire household. I, too, had a tin helmet and drove a mobile canteen, passing out hot coffee and sandwiches to air-raid wardens on duty. My father and I left the house for our posts and my mother quickly pushed the two old ladies out of their beds and shepherded them to the small, dark storeroom under the stairs which we called the Black Hole. This manoeuvre, too, had its precision drill. There was just room in the Hole for one complete old lady, and the front—slimmer—half of another one. And so Nana and Juliet took it turn and turn about: five minutes exposure to the expected bombardment of the one billowing, bed-robed behind which could not be squeezed under cover—and then—panting, pulling and manipulating, my mother turned them about. Whenever, in France, I see plump pink *poulets-de-Bresse* being turned on a spit, my mind dwells not on the feast ahead of me, but on the memory of Nana and Juliet being turned in the Hole. Not one bomb was ever dropped on Sydney, but the air-raid drill gave considerable zest to the old ladies' nocturnal hours.

It also gave my father the idea of trying to frighten Aunt Juliet to death, as neither nature nor the Japanese seemed likely to finish her off for a great many years, and I was then her main beneficiary when the end came. I doubt whether his intentions were serious, for he had no real animosity towards her; but the carrying out of his plan amused him.

At the time, our chief resident guest was my particular acquisition: a young, beautiful, and high-spirited Russian boy, Nicki Ivangin. Nicki was a dancer, a member of Colonel de Basil's Monte Carlo Ballet Company and, at nineteen, had been washed up

on our doorstep by war, a broken leg, and the pre-
cipitous departure of the Company while he was still
encased in plaster. I, hopelessly in love, brought him
home one day, and my father took delight in
embellishing Nicki's English with Australian phrases.
Nicki's stock answer to any opinion soon became,
'D'you reckon?' He was an appreciative and encour-
aging audience to my father and entered with glee
into rehearsals for the terrorising of Juliet.

Her room was built at the bend of the stairway
linking ground floor to first, and opposite her
bedroom door was a small window leading on to a
narrow shaft, called, in those days—for it seems since
to have vanished from modern houses —a 'light area'.
My father and Nicki, practising when Juliet was out of
the house, perfected a deafening series of explosions
by dropping electric light bulbs down the light area
from the roof. My father was to start dropping and the
first bang was the signal for Nicki to charge, suitably
dressed and yelling, into Juliet's bedroom. In the tin
helmet, heavy Oriental make-up around his Slav eyes,
a 1914-vintage Sam Browne of my uncle's, and
brandishing an old naval sword of my father's, he
looked macabre enough for the job. It didn't kill Aunt
Juliet, but it scared her half out of her already feeble

wits. And it took days to clean the splinters of ground light bulbs from the area.

As the war went on, food and clothing became comparatively scarce, even in Australia. There was no actual shortage, but certain foodstuffs were rationed, and all clothing. My parents accepted these restrictions as a challenge to their ingenuity in obtaining them. My mother's attentions and ministrations to all the tradespeople and shopkeepers in our vicinity, always intense, became positively overwhelming. Children's birthdays were remembered, jobs found for adolescent and ageing members of the various Greek and Italian families, partnerships entered into for the buying of joint lottery tickets, free medical attention from my father, with which she had always been prolific, was practically forced on reasonably healthy adults. The occasional fillet steak with which these attentions were rewarded was forgotten as the end in my mother's whole-hearted absorption and enjoyment in the means: she appreciated the affection and dependence of her small colony of suppliers more than we did the fruits of her efforts.

Our current maid, Phyllis, was a tough and sly little character who rapidly did less and less housework and more and more of the duties of a bookmaking clerk for my mother. She knew all the jockeys and racing tipsters and was deeply involved in the war-time black market.

My mother quickly discovered this potential source of supply and substituted a telephone for the broom in Phyllis' hand. My mother did the sweeping while Phyllis ferreted out racing form and Lucky Strikes. She, like all our servants, developed a passionate attachment to my mother, and a detached and impersonal hatred of the unknown aunts, whom she hounded from a distance whenever the opportunity presented. The poor old ladies received a telephone call from Phyllis one day.

'This is the Parcels Office at Central Railway Station. There's a crate of eggs addressed to you here waiting to be picked up.'

A crate of eggs was an extraordinary windfall— Litter, Titter, Fritter and Anus clustered round the telephone in amazement.

'Good heavens,' said Anus, the youngest and most aggressive, 'where on earth have they come from?'

'From a hen's arsehole, of course,' said Phyllis, and hung up.

My father's concern was solely with the clothing of his own person and he soon stumbled on the simplest way of achieving this. Each young man whom I brought home for dinner or a drink was immediately asked to which branch of the services he was attached—those on combat duty being rejected out of hand, and those in the Services of Supply being retained on the end of a reasonably civil conversational string on their chances of having a connection with the Quartermaster's Office. But if they were foolish enough to come right out with the statement that they were in the Q.M.'s Department, then my father pounced. Placing a proprietary hand on my shoulder and pushing the whisky decanter towards the victim, he would deem the hook sufficiently baited to announce, 'I'm very short of underpants.' For some time after the Americans had gone home and left us to the much less affluent British Navy, and even after the war had ended, my father's cupboards looked like an overflow from a P.X. store. Other girls in war-time Sydney dripped with orchids and were fed regularly on champagne and caviar. I had to make do with roses and sparkling burgundy, as supplying father loomed large on the budget of many of my escorts.

In addition to the countless young men who were fresh fodder for either his teasing or his shock tactics, my father delighted in any suitably unsophisticated

female friends I was able to provide. A positive
windfall to him was the fact that my two most intimate
friends were virgin soil—one a young refugee from
New Guinea whose family had been trapped by the
Japanese and the other a Dutch ballet dancer evacu-
ated on the last boat out of Java—both exceptionally
pretty and therefore offering many more opportunities
for exploitation. Pauline had been educated by nuns
and had won points for good behaviour by a system of
pin pricks on a board which, when added up, earned
the children the doubtful privilege of 'adopting' an
orphaned native baby. 'Ten pricks get you a black
baby,' she told my father. This was good for endless
parties. He waited until Pauline was suitably
surrounded by as many respectable matrons as could
be gathered, before prompting, 'Tell them how you
get a black baby, Pauline, how you have to have had
ten pricks.'

Edmeé, the Dutch ballet dancer, learnt most of her
English from my father. He carefully coached her in
polite cocktail party conversation before her first visit
to Government House.

'Now just say to any young man you are introduced
to: "I hear there are a lot of trouser snakes around
here." That will get the ball rolling.' Most of his

adages sounded particularly weird, if not positively fetching, in Edmeé's heavily accented vowels.

When the Americans set up a permanent base in Sydney, I became the secretary of the Commanding Officer of the Ordnance Department. At the Ammunition Depot some miles out of Sydney where we worked for a time, there were frequent opportunities to procure off-ration foodstuffs. Cream and eggs could be bought from surrounding farmers, and plentiful chickens. Our go-between was an old porter who moved the ammunition boxes between the storage sheds when he wasn't conducting a one-man farmers' market among the personnel. Fred came sidling up to me one day.

'Interested in buying a pig, miss?'

'A pig! Alive or dead?'

'Well,' said Fred, 'it's alive now, but I've got a Major over in Transportation who says he'll take half, and if I can settle for the other half, the farmer says he'll kill one next full moon.'

The killing at full moon was no tribal ritual, but as local consumption of bacon was prohibited and all war-time pigs reared for overseas bacon export, it was impossible to break the law so openly in daylight. I knew the thought of buying a whole (or half) pig

would instantly appeal to my mother, so I telephoned her while Fred waited.

'How big?' she wanted to know, and 'How much?'

Fred thought about sixty pounds and about a fiver. My mother was thrilled: she got the butcher to agree to house her half of the pig in his freezer and she managed to off-load several pounds of pork in advance to some of her friends. After that she settled down to planning a series of pork parties and the packing of an unprecedented number of hampers for her troops. A positive fever of expectancy gripped our office as pig-killing day drew near. Fred occasionally gave me bulletins on the animal's health: I had had to take my boss into my confidence because of transportation difficulties and he had kindly promised to drive me and the pig back to town in his staff car on the day. Two days before the appointed night, the Major in Transportation pulled out of his half of the deal. Fred came to me in distress: but by now I knew my mother was sure to see little difference between half a pig and a whole pig, so we became sole owners.

My father; Edmeé Cameron (*née* Monod), my Dutch dancer friend; and 'Blackie' (Frederick Blackman), the man who came to dinner and stayed seventeen years.

Pig-killing night was fine and clear. The next morning, Fred was gleefully conspiratorial.

'Oh, a lovely pig you've got there, miss. He's over in the bushes behind Transportation. A fine 120-pound pig. But you'd better get him out quick before the M.P.s come around.'

No city-bred person who has never bought a pig can possibly visualise the difference between an expected sixty-pounder and the solid reality of a 120-pound pig. There he lay—stretched in pink and unlovely grandeur, stark among the bushes. He had wispy grey hair, long enough to plait. He was obviously, prior to death, a very old pig. There was no time for recriminations: there was no question of my being able to get him out quick without considerable help. My understanding boss detailed two staff sergeants and a lorry to help me; they managed to manipulate the stiff and hideous beast into the back of a truck, cover it with a tarpaulin and drive it, and myself, into town. We got the truck as close as possible to our back door, for there was now no question of delivering this naked corpse direct to the busy butcher's shop in broad daylight, as had been planned with half his lighter predecessor. The sergeants got him through the back door, dumped him on my grandmother's hall carpet, and left.

My grandmother felt her Jewish background should cause her to register a rueful protest at her carpet being made the repository for a dead pig, and all afternoon she harassed us as, sweating, my mother and I hacked the creature into transportable pieces with surgical instruments and wrapped them, dripping with blood, in newspaper. When we had made several trips across the road with the pieces, the butcher shook his head sadly and told us that this ancient animal was good for nothing except bacon, and that he'd be willing to pay my mother two or three pounds for it to turn into bacon. The following morning I had to hand over fourteen pounds to Fred.

The shortage of alcohol, too, was a spur to invention. My father concocted a sort of house drink, which had an innocuous taste and a quite spectacular effect. He made it in a huge china punch-bowl, big enough to take a couple of bottles at a time without splashing, or the boredom of measuring, and though its basic ingredient was rum, its component parts varied according to what happened to be available. But whatever the ingredients, the name remained the same, a name to become famous throughout the South West Pacific—'Bunsby Gaze'.

The original Bunsby Gaze was a racehorse of no particular merit, but whose form my father had been following and in whose performance he had had reason to be disappointed. The first time he mixed the drink he decided that its taste and colour was to be imaginatively compared to the taste of horse's urine— not a very good horse—in fact, Bunsby Gaze. Long after the horse had ceased to race, Bunsby Gazes were still being remembered with nostalgia in the New Guinea jungles.

Sundays became, through the slow building up of habit and war-time commitments, our chief 'at home' day. There were never less than twelve for Sunday lunch and usually twenty or thirty for Sunday supper. My father and I and the hard resident core went to the beach every Sunday morning, while my mother prepared her enormous meals. By evening, the Bunsby Gazes were flowing and when my father thought his audience was in a sufficiently receptive mood he did his imitation. This was of Ronald Colman. It involved no speech or action: the characterisation was simply in my father's concept of the unfortunate man whom he had seen on the screen only once and who appeared to him to have, for a screen idol, extremely short legs. He also found him singularly lacking in facial expression.

Bondi, 1939.

He stuck a burnt match moustache on his face and, hat and overcoat on, he took up his position kneeling behind the curtains (with which my mother was gradually replacing the doors in as many rooms as she could get her hands on). I then announced the act, pulled the curtains, and there knelt my father on Ronald Colman's short legs, glaring at the audience with a fierce and fixed expression. After one minute he turned and hobbled away. This regularly reduced people who had seen it week after week to tears of laughter, so he saw no reason why he should vary the act. After he shot himself, he could no longer get down on his knees, so that was the end of Ronald Colman.

My father as Ronald Colman.

CHAPTER 12

Perhaps because I was an only child and a precocious one, there was no distinction made between the generations in our household. My parents' friends were my friends, and my friends became, equally, friends of my parents. All topics were discussed in front of me, and only in the presence of an overwhelming majority of young people did my mother strive to be conscious of some division in age groups. One evening she was discussing, with a contemporary, a newly arrived theatrical producer on the Sydney scene. Four or five of my young friends were listening and my father was stretched, eyes closed, in his corner chair. The man was, thought my mother, a bad producer.

'In fact,' she said, 'he's not a producer's ...' remembering, not quite in the nick of time, her audience, '... boot hole!'

This extraordinary epithet would have gone unnoticed had not my father opened one eye to correct her. 'Arse lace you mean, dear.'

My father derived great amusement out of the U.S. troops with whom he came, through me, in contact. They were perfect tease material, and he was, above all, a tease. On the whole, they were in and out of our lives so fast that he had some difficulty in distinguishing one from the other; however, I did manage, in the rush, to become engaged to two of them, and he had, perforce, to establish the identity of these two who might conceivably have become his sons-in-law. The first was a strapping young airman, with flashing teeth, who rejoiced in the unforgettably splendid name of Joshua H. Barnes, the Fifth. His home town was Paris, Kentucky, and my father's tease was of a subversive nature, being directed at me rather than at Josh. He solemnly told all visitors, 'You know Robin's fiancé never had boots on till he joined the Army.'

After Josh, came Torbert H. Macdonald. Torbert was in P.T. boats, much more sophisticated, and visited Sydney often enough to become firm friends

with my father. He had played football for Harvard—my father had played football for Melbourne University—and this formed the basis of their endless wrangles. Together they went to matches played under Australian Rules, my father explaining the rules and Torbert proclaiming the superiority of the American game. This argument always ended by my father snorting, 'American football! Why, you wear so much padding that when you fall down the umpire has to shoot you!'

Torbert fell into the tease mould in every way, even to getting himself heavily decorated while on P.T. patrol, including a Purple Heart for having got his ankle caught in a mooring rope. On the leave following this injury, my father evolved his own decoration for Torbert. He had a medal made for him, a large round plaque on which was engraved a mosquito in full flight, poised above the numbers 106. The medal was bright yellow and was called the Malarial Medal. On the back the citation read, 'For having reached the temperature of 106 degrees during an attack of Malaria and survived'.

(*above*) During the war with fiancé no. 1, airman Joshua H. Barnes, here at Romano's, 1942. (*below*) Fiancé no. 2, Torbert Macdonald.

He found the British Navy, when they arrived, more difficult to tease, but easier to shock: this amused him just as much. I was getting on splendidly with a Lieutenant Commander in aircraft carriers until the day my father produced one of his medical books and handed it around, open at a photograph of a diseased male organ.

'Have you ever seen Robin's Aunt Bertie?' he said. 'Here's a picture of her. She's downstairs now if you'd care to see her; you'll recognise her by this, except that she's got a hat on now.'

The photograph was, I regret to say, almost a speaking likeness, if one half-closed one's eyes, of my dear Aunt Bertie. She was the one of my grand-mother's married sisters with whom we had remained on the most friendly terms, a splendidly robust old character, but she did possess a most unfortunate nose. My friendship, however, with the naval officer petered out.

CHAPTER 13

I have, in an old album, a photograph taken during
the war, and under it I have written in explanation
of the strange assortment of faces staring at the camera,
'Errol's Farewell'. It is a large group photograph, ten
of us arranged in varying attitudes of admiration and
motley collection of garments around a grinning
photograph on an easel. Lying in the foreground is my
mother, looking exceedingly alarmed and grasping a
large hambone in one hand. Other friends have put on
hats and dresses which they had found at random in her
cupboards; my father is in his Ronald Colman outfit; a
sailor friend is dressed as a woman and I have on his
sailor suit; and, clutching his arm, is the maid Phyllis,
stuffed with pillows and daubed with paint. I cannot

remember any directing thought behind our dressing-
up for this photograph. I can only remember that we
hired the photographer for a fee of three guineas from
a local newspaper and that he remained stunned by
disbelief and alcohol far into the night. We wanted it as
a farewell present for Errol, the friend after whom our
cat was named, who was on the eve of departure to
India. It was a sort of peace-offering, for my father had
recently been responsible for Errol's spending some
hours in the custody of the Security Police.

Some years earlier, Errol had had some portraits
taken, and had given us one: he was a gay and
pleasant-looking man, but in black-and-white looked
like an easter egg on which a grin and glasses had been
painted. We had put it away in a drawer, and, in a war-
time clean out, I had happened upon this fatuous face.
Errol was now drafted from his peace-time occupation
in shipping, and had a highly secret job on Garden
Island, Sydney's central naval dockyard. We knew this
job had something to do with shipping movements:
apart from that, we knew only the personal anecdotes
about his colleagues with which Errol occasionally
entertained us. He appeared to be waging a weekly
vendetta with a spinster of uncertain age, a Miss
Harrison, who was the Admiral's secretary, and

almost every Sunday he had some fresh tale to add
to demonstrate Miss Harrison's eccentricity. After
some weeks, the lady started telephoning my father,
in his capacity as Port Medical Officer, and pestering
him with requests and suggestions for the use of the
girls on her naval secretarial staff in his dockside
medical posts. Her attentions became so persistent
and so odd that he began to suspect a plan between
Errol and the lady to tease him. 'I believe she's a
perfectly ordinary and sane woman,' he said. 'She
must be to hold down her job. Errol's put her up to
this.'

The photograph provided him with what he

FOLLOWING PAGES: Giving Errol the 'V for Victory'
farewell. (*back from left to right*) Michael Cadell, in some of
my mother's clothes; Phyllis, the maid; Eve Ramsden, a
journalist friend who supplied the photographer; 'Blackie';
Sigrid Clerici (wife of Tony Clerici, maitre d' at Romano's);
Audrey Maiden, the funniest of my mother's friends; Billie
Styles, wife of leading actor Edwin Styles, in one of my
dresses; Tiger Cadell, a close family friend and mother of
the two Cadell boys. (*front*) Edmée; me in Mike Cadell's
sailor suit; Jim Cadell; my mother clutching a hambone; my
flatmate, Libby Watson. My father, as Ronald Colman,
kneels in the centre above Errol's photograph.

thought was the perfect opportunity for a counter-
tease. He typed on a slip of paper—'WARNING.
WHEN THE JAPS COME TAKE YOUR ORDERS
FROM THIS MAN'—and with this pasted beneath
the grinning face, he posted it off to the unknown
Miss Harrison.

Miss Harrison was the Admiral's secretary all right:
she had been perfectly serious in her telephone calls to
my father; she was no friend of Errol's; she had no
sense of humour, or, after contemplating that bland
smile above the incongruous message, no sense of the
ridiculous. She scurried straight off to the Security
Office and turned over the evidence to them. Poor
Errol was called up and asked if he had had some
photographs taken recently, to whom he had given
them, and on failing to remember, was asked about his
Germanic middle name and his frequent pre-war
travelling on behalf of his shipping company. They
released him by nightfall, but his dossier went into
Security files.

Not long afterwards he was transferred, and my
father, who had confessed, had 'our' photograph
mounted as a farewell gesture.

His other war-time prank, of equal magnitude,
remained undetected. He poisoned, in a mild but
discomforting way, a girl called Libby, with whom

I shared a flat. The flat was my first venture into freedom, and Libby and I were both allowed to live in it, provided we lived with each other. Libby's father was a country doctor, and we were working in the same U.S. Army office. We also ate all our meals, including breakfast, at my family's house, and our 'freedom' did not even involve washing our own clothes. All the more irritating chores of domestic life were still taken care of for us by my mother.

One night I was awakened by desperate groans. Libby, in her nightdress, was lurching about the room in which we both slept, bumping, albeit gently, into the furniture, and clutching her abdomen. Every now and then she gave a tiny shriek, grabbed a cushion from a chair, dropped it on the floor, and carefully fell on it. There she kicked and rolled and jerked, shrieking and groaning and frightening me to distraction. I soothed her as best I could and, having thrust myself into some clothes, ran the three blocks to my father. He got up, dressed, and came back with me. Libby had made herself reasonably comfortable on her pillows and smiled wanly up at him. I paced the bathroom while he examined her and gave her an injection—expecting an emergency appendix at least. Libby had a 'grumbling' appendix: this heightened our sense of gravity. It seemed, however, that all that ailed Libby was a severe pain of perfectly natural origin, and for which she must have, by experience, been well prepared. After that, Libby's monthly pains got first me, and then my father, out of bed on two more occasions: the second time he arrived to find her calmly asleep in my bed.

On the third and last time, he gave her, instead of an injection, some pills. The following morning was a beautiful, bright Sunday. Our usual party, including a fully recovered Libby, were setting out for the beach when my father drew Libby aside and advised her to stay quietly at home helping my mother with the lunch. After all, she had had, he pointed out, a disturbed night. We spent a blissfully peaceful morning which seemed surprisingly more so because of the absence of Libby's undeniably whining voice.

Around one o'clock my father stretched luxuriously on the hot sand. 'We'd better get home to your poor mother. I imagine she's had a busy morning with Libby.'

Of course he had done something outrageous. Even without the tone in his voice and the gleam in his eye there was something anticipatory in his very stretch. Pressed, he admitted it: Libby's pills had been the strongest dose of laxative he had felt could safely be given. She was unable to go to the office for two days: she never got my father out of bed again, and

I don't think she ever suspected what he had done.

During the war it was almost impossible to find anyone to do house repairs, and so our house gradually began to fall apart. The roof was totally inadequate, and at each tropical storm we ran with basins and buckets from the kitchen to catch the drips, which steadily grew into torrents. My father once solved the problem of a bulging and waterlogged patch by drilling a hole through it. The water obligingly channelled itself through this in a single jet, directly above the middle of my mother's bed. She once set off down the stairs for a gala premiere, suitably bejewelled, skirts held high over the soggy floorboards, with umbrella aloft. This was during a storm of such tropical fury that Amy's black legs and arms whirled between bucket and window—bailing— and my mother swore her face turned white with fright that night.

Maramanah, during the 1940s, was the first landmark in our lives to go. One night I was awakened by my mother jigging with excitement, to the noise of fire engines clanging down our street.

'Quick! Get out of bed,' she commanded. 'Maramanah's on fire—let's go and watch.'

Down the street we pelted: she always loved a good fire anyway, and as she rarely went to bed, the fact

that it was two in the morning was no deterrent to
her enjoyment. Indeed, it was an exceptionally bright
blaze: the towers and turrets and iron-laced balconies
showed up beautifully, and my mother was only disappointed that there was no sign of the aunts being
lowered by ropes. We went back in the morning to
view the damage, and for the first time, I was allowed
inside the blackened rooms in which I had wandered
so many times in imagination, accompanied by my
grandmother's ghosts.

I had such a vivid picture of some of the rooms that
it was a dreadful disappointment to see them, so banal,
and so empty. I could not, for one moment, suppose
that all my ten aunts had slept in one enormous bed,
and yet I could not erase from my mind the picture
of them all, under an acre of blanket, which my
grandmother had undoubtedly planted there. She
had, I swear, told me that there was a 'bed' leader,
who commanded, at intervals throughout the night,
'Turn!', and turn they did, in unison, so that they
should not be breathing germs down each other's
throats. Perhaps, I now wonder, was it the four
unmarried ones who huddled thus for company,
while their sisters lay in germ-filled and connubial
imprecision in nearby rooms? But why? There was
ample space in the house, and ample money, for

separate beds. I do not know: the bed drill sticks, unchallenged in my memory, along with the green apples and the balloon, as family legend.

I expected, too, to feel at least the aura of my great-grandfather's benevolent personality as I had had it so often described to me. He had seemed such a genial and loving man in such satisfyingly concrete ways that I wanted some evidence of his presence to embrace me. Two of my grandmother's anecdotes about him had endeared him to me—once when my mother was a small girl and was scolded by her nurse for standing under a garden hose in her new red shoes, he bundled the sobbing child into his carriage and they went shopping for an identical pair.

'There you are,' he said, 'one pair is specially to wear under the hose if you feel so inclined.'

I daresay it wasn't the best way to train a child, but it must have been one of the nicest possible childhood recollections for my mother. And, as his children grew older, his remedy for any tears was to send to the cellar for a bottle of champagne to cheer them up.

After the fire, the aunts never went back. They settled in an apartment nearby, and one night six families of 'squatters' moved into Maramanah with mattresses, babies and primus stoves, and there they stayed until finally ejected by the local council. The council then managed to coax the old ladies to sell the site, and it is now a fairly handsome park and children's playground.

Somehow, the aunts in an apartment no longer afforded the challenge that they had while brooding at the end of the street, and my grandmother's visits to them grew rarer. Although Nana, in later years, remained almost permanently in bed, she also remained in full command of her surroundings. It was frustrating and pointless to struggle against her will in any matter on which she was already determined. My father had wrested a kind of negative victory from his private battles with her, but not for long did anyone else's opposition prevail. One of the most abject surrenders which I remember was the Tax Inspector's.

Thirteen years after my grandfather died, it was discovered, quite by accident, that Nana had never entered a tax return. Everyone tried to explain to her why this should have been done, and to extract from her some plausible excuse as to why it had not. Her excuse was quite simple—she had never heard of such a thing and nobody had bothered to tell her. If the affair had not already reached the level of the lowest cubicle in the hierarchy of tax assessors, the family would have kept quiet and done nothing—the back liability of thirteen years being too vast to contemplate as an actually present problem to be tackled. But it was out of our hands, and too late. After my mother had had her session, the family doctor tried: then various business friends, and finally her bank manager—all seated by her bedside, explaining gently in a concili-atory tone the basic principles of paying one's taxes. My grandmother plainly thought them all lacking in elementary common sense.

'But how,' she demanded, 'can I pay something I haven't got? I would gladly do so if there really were any money left over, but I spend all my income and, what is more, I spend it all on other people. So I don't see how I can possibly find this excess sum. You have only to look at my bank statements to see on what necessities I have spent it.'

Meanwhile, the paper work in the Inland Revenue Department had been mounting, and demand notes being of no avail, her bank manager spoke in person to the Collector of Taxes. It was decided that in view of the fact that she was then eighty-nine, and seldom rose from her bed, the Collector would take his turn at her bedside.

Nobody else was present at this interview. It lasted two hours, and at the end of it he came out red in the face and mopping his brow.

'It's no good,' he admitted. 'She's an old lady and we'll just have to wait till she dies.'

And wait they did, another four years, while Nana remained smug and secure in the belief that common sense had won the day.

Nana and Juliet and Bertie spoke on the telephone every day. The two old ladies had the telephone on the table between their beds, and usually took it in turns to talk to Bertie, relaying the conversation between sentences in shouts across to the other bed. I remember once bringing a schoolfriend in to see my grandmother. She was a new friend and so my grandmother was delighted to have such fresh conversational opportunity. We stayed chatting for some twenty minutes before Nana leaned half out of bed to reach the ginger jar she kept on her table. I caught a fleeting glimpse of something black in the bed where her body had been. This black object was making a queer muffled, rasping noise.

'Nana,' I said, backing away, 'there's something in your bed and I think it's alive.'

'Oh, dear God!' she cried, 'It's Bertie!'

It was Bertie—on the telephone. She was reading the *Sydney Morning Herald*'s leader column aloud, and was blissfully unaware that she had been talking to the wrong end of her sister.

As she and Juliet grew older and more bedridden, Nana finally succumbed to one of the many requests to let off part of her house, and her drawing-room and dining-room became an estate agency. Considerable reconstruction was needed, and this was carried out in a fine spirit of optimism by the tenants, as she refused to sign a lease. Every year, the manager hopefully presented himself with the lease ready for signature and every year she sent him away, saying, 'My father told me never to sign anything I didn't understand and I don't understand a word of this. Mr Briggs, my word is my bond.'

After the war ended, the life of the house weakened and slowly died. First, the troops left, and the Sunday parties shrank. Nicki, now able to rejoin his parents in Paris, and I, aching to join my latest beau in England, sat around waiting for transport out of Australia. What had remained a constant twosome throughout the war years was now a trio: we had been joined by a painter, Wolf Kardamatis—half-Greek, half-German—stranded too in Australia by the war. The three of us played endless games of cards with my mother and haunted the airline and shipping companies.

Nicki, beautiful Nicki, already at twenty-three dying bravely of a fatal disease, wanted only to see his Russian parents and his Paris once more. Wolf had never wanted to come to Australia in the first place. His German mother had died at his birth, and his

Greek grandmother had brought him up in Athens. When Wolf was fifteen, his immigrant father in Australia had sent for him. Wolf locked himself in a lavatory in Port Said and the ship sailed on without him: he conducted a flourishing business at his subsequent Sydney public school in hand-painted copies of the dirty postcards he'd picked up there while waiting for the next ship. Expelled, he had gone on to art school and, when in the first feverish week of war a formation of planes had flown overhead at a crowded cocktail party, Wolf rushed to the window and shouted, 'Mein Fuehrer! Mein Fuehrer! Don't shoot! It's only me!' Born in Berlin, he still had his German passport, but in disgrace next morning he was taken by his father to be naturalised. His passport was the only Australian thing about him: he remained permanently rebellious in an alien culture, but in our house he created a small Greek corner for himself.

We left within a week of each other—the boys on a ship and I hitchhiking on a converted bomber. My parents made no attempt to stop me leaving. They tried, as they always had, to help me live my life to its fullest stretching point.

A last look over the shoulder at Australia before leaving for Europe.

But that was the beginning of the house's decline. For a year or two, my mother had enormous fun with food parcels: my friends in England were inundated. Mine usually had a bottle of whisky, well padded by marshmallows, tucked inside. To test it, she stood on the dining-room table and hurled it to the floor: if the whisky didn't break, she deemed it sufficiently padded to brave the post. At a Christmas house party in England, when all the other guests had had their quota of tins from my mother, Harold French and I composed a cable to her, silly with Christmas spirit: 'Please send Harold French parcel. He's old, silly, but rather nice and has never had a parcel.'

My mother's answering cable said: 'Of course, darling, but who is Harold and what is a French parcel?'

Meanwhile she'd been shopping, in a bewildered way, for all the champignons, *pâté de foie gras* and truffles she could find. I lived in England for four years before my mother died but her letters came daily and I, knowing her nocturnal habits, could picture her at the round dining table, patience cards and empty tea cups pushed aside, cigarette butts mounting up, writing far into the night. My father acquired a nurse, Peggy, shortly after I left, and Peggy increasingly filled the pages in my mother's letters—not with a happy note but with uncharacteristic resentment. Peggy was always upstairs, Peggy had been rude to her— insulting—and the worst aspect of all this was that my father had upheld Peggy against his wife. The daily saga went on for weeks and I skimmed over this boring tirade until finally it dawned on me that perhaps the root of my mother's distress was a suspicion that my father was actually having an affair with this usurper, and that she was trying to tell me this in a gentle, indeed genteel way. Alarmed, I wrote back to ask her if this was the case. 'Don't be silly,' she wrote back. 'Of course not. He's seen far too many twots better looking than her face.' In no way could I afterwards visualise the unseen Peggy as a threat.

In another year she was dead. Then Aunt Juliet. When Aunt Juliet was killed by the bus, although my grandmother, then over ninety, lived to link me with the past by her still wonderful letters, the secure, magic place of my childhood vanished with her. My father broke the news to me, in England, by a cable: 'JULIET SKITTLED,' it said. 'LOVE, DAD.'

Only he and my grandmother remained, unspeaking, in the lonely house.

Lastly, outliving all her loved ones, my grandmother

died. The house was sold. The new owners were the long-suffering estate agents who were my grandmother's tenants. The rooms became offices, dress shops, coffee bars; the front was all plate-glass and the roof was renewed. In the fullness of time and progress these gave way in turn to a sex arcade and now an underground station. And, as a final gesture to conformity, the tree has been uprooted from the Cross.